Sid Sackson

A GAMUT of GAMES

with drawings by the author

Hutchinson

London Melbourne Sydney Auckland Johannesburg

This book is dedicated to Bernice—
Because she was always available
to test a game, to offer advice and,
when necessary, criticism.
Because she typed a rough manuscript
under an impossible deadline.
And above all because she has put up
with a game nut for all these years.

Hutchinson & Co. (Publishers) Ltd
An imprint of the Hutchinson Publishing Group
17-21 Conway Street, London W1P 6JD

Hutchinson Group (Australia) Pty Ltd
30-32 Cremorne Street, Richmond South, Victoria 3121
PO Box 151, Broadway, New South Wales 2007

Hutchinson Group (NZ) Ltd
32-34 View Road, PO Box 40-086, Glenfield, Auckland 10

Hutchinson Group (SA) Pty Ltd
PO Box 337, Bergvlei 2012, South Africa

First published 1969
Second edition 1982
First published in Great Britain as a
Hutchinson Paperback 1983

Printed and bound in Great Britain by
Anchor Brendon Ltd
Tiptree, Essex

British Library Cataloguing in Publication Data
Sackson, Sid
  A gamut of games
  1. Indoor games
  I. Title
  793   GV1229
ISBN 0 09 153340 6 Cased
ISBN 0 09 153341 4 Hutchinson Paperback

Preface to the Second Edition

In thirteen years much has happened—and much has remained the same. On a sad note, Lech Pijanowski, Haar Hoolim, and Arthur Amberstone have died. Wald, Arthur's son, has drifted away from games. On a happier note, Father Daniel has been released from his vows, has married, and is the proud father of two. This, and his continuing ties to the order, leave him little time for games.

Alex Randolph is now based in Venice and flies here occasionally. His prodigious output continues, including MOONSTAR and PUSH OVER, which have also crossed the Atlantic. Jim Dunnigan, having severed his connections to the publishing house he helped to found, is now a consultant to the government and the author of several books on wargaming and war itself. Bob Abbott has expanded CROSSINGS into the attractive EPAMINONDAS, available in England, Germany, and the United States. His game creativity is now focused on the computer.

Claude Soucie and I are all that really remains of N.Y.G.A. At his request I have corrected an error in the rules for LINES OF ACTION, eliminating possible draws. The game has, with good reason, attracted a following among lovers of strategic games. Phil Laurence hasn't come up with any new games, but he and Annette are as generously helpful as ever in playing mine. Their daughter Jill has joined us— and usually wins.

Felicia Parker remains my friend and agent. Through her I found another friend, and overseas agent—Bill Riva. Their efforts resulted in FOCUS being produced in Germany, where I had the thrill of accepting an award from a government minister when it was chosen as "game of the year" for 1981. It is now available in the United States under the name DOMINATION.

In 1970 I gave up my job as an engineer to devote myself to creating games, writing on games, and nourishing the collection. Some wonderful new friends—including Walter Luc Haas in Switzerland and Derek Carver and Eamon Bloomfield in England—have been most helpful with European contributions. Actually, the collection threatens to push us from our home; but through it all Bernice continues to put up with a game nut, and I am eternally grateful.

SID SACKSON
July 1982

Preface

IN ANY BOOKSTORE you can find many collections of games, most with the name "Hoyle" somewhere in the title. And there are many games in each collection. The searcher after something different, however, finds the same games, like old friends, reappearing in all the collections, sometimes in slightly varied dress and sometimes with a new name.

The purpose of this book is to present a selection of games, thirty-eight it turns out, that will not be found in the "Hoyles," either because they were invented by my friends and me or because they are old—but good—games that somehow have gotten lost in the shuffle.

The games were chosen not only because they are different but also to fulfill some function not adequately satisfied by the standard games. You will find a completely novel game of strategy played on a checkerboard by partners; a two-hand POKER game that can be played for fun instead of money; a really satisfying substitute for two stranded BRIDGE players; a number of replacements for the soporific TIC-TAC-TOE; a card game of pure and brain-stretching skill; a rare game of inductive logic played with pencil and paper; and many others. (Now might be a good time for a quick tour through the table of contents.) You will also find games created by a Polish film critic, a Benedictine monk, two basket weavers, a retired Israeli "student," and a historian who explores the origins of World War I.

It would be too much to expect that every game will appeal to every reader, but it will be a rare reader who won't find several games that he really likes and at least one that he loves.

I haven't made too much of an effort to be consistent in the method of presenting the games; I prefer to let each one dictate its own form (heeding the advice of one of my professors who insisted that "consistency is the bugaboo of small minds"). I have, however, made every effort to see that each game is complete and clear, with the necessary diagrams and examples to make it easy to follow.

Although this volume is by no means intended as a history of games, I have included a liberal sprinkling of historical information and contemporary comment in an effort to show where these particular games belong in the general universe of games.

I WAS NOT AWARE of it at the time, but I began preparing for this book when I was in first grade. The high point of a school day would occur when the teacher distributed pages from a magazine and instructed us to circle the words we knew. The positioning of the circles and their relationship to each other interested me much more than the words themselves. I evolved rules for joining the circles, set objectives for the growing chains, and thereby created my first game.

A little later I was presented with an UNCLE WIGGILY game. Almost immediately I began expanding upon the included rules. First I increased the number of rabbits per player and allowed them to be captured and returned to their starting point (unknowingly reinventing PARCHEESI). Before long the captures became more important than the race, the pieces changed from rabbits to soldiers and cannons, and full-fledged wars were being waged under the noses of Dr. Possum, the Bad Pipsisewah, and the Skillery Scallery Alligator.

The next profound influence was a LOTTO set purchased with my own savings. The game itself was disappointingly dull, but there was a compensation. Included with the game was a check sheet upon which the ninety numbered discs were placed as they were drawn. The grouping of these discs reminded me of the mapped growth of empires in the history books. The next step was to divide the sheet into the countries of Europe and to create my own history. The beauty of this game was that it could be played by one. A lonely kid uprooted from city after city by a father in search of employment during the 1930s filled many an otherwise empty hour watching empires rise and fall, including the time when Finland conquered all of Europe.

From the same inspiration of the grouped discs there later came the idea of forming hotel chains, enlarging them, and merging them. This, with the addition of stock and money, became my game of ACQUIRE which is currently one of the 3M Bookshelf Games.

Now, some forty-three years after my initial discovery of games in the first grade, I am just as intrigued by what makes a game tick as I was then. I have created several hundred games of my own (twenty-two of which are included in this volume), but I am just as fascinated by one created by a friend, one I buy in a store, or one I rediscover in a library or museum. With this as a spur, my collection of games and books on games (in eight languages) has grown to be what is, to the best of my knowledge, the largest privately owned collection.

Drawing upon this amassed information, I have prepared a section of the book devoted to short reviews of the games currently available in the stores. In this age of sealed packages ∘nd self-service such a review is a must for the potential purchaser of a game. To cover every game, including the thousands of repetitious children's games, would take several volumes the size of this one and would be of little value. The types of games covered—and those omitted—are described in the introduction to the review section.

I want to convey my sincerest thanks to the following. If it weren't for them, not only would this book not have been finished; it would never have been started.

—Annette and Phil Laurence, who helped in testing just about every game in the book. Phil, in addition, contributed a card game which could easily be the start of a new craze.

—Claude Soucie, Bob Abbott, Arthur and Wald Amberstone, my fellow New York Game Associates (N.Y.G.A. for short), whose stimulating company sparked so many of my creative fires, and who each supplied me with an irreplaceable game.

—Haar Hoolim, Father Daniel, Lech Pijanowski, and Alex Randolph, whose inspiring companionship came through the mails. It is with pleasure and pride that I present a game from each of them.

—Jim Dunnigan who, though I have known him for barely a year, insisted on creating a unique game expressly for this book.

—Felicia Parker and the late Alice Nichols, two brilliant and creative women, my agents, and my dear friends, who kept me trying through the long, lean years.

—My father, an amateur linguist, who helped me over all the language barriers.

—My children, Dana and Dale, who really don't like games very much. But when the chips were down they were always there to help. And their final reading of the manuscript caught many an error that might otherwise have slipped through.

—My wife, Bernice.

If you have any comments—or any questions—concerning the games, letters sent through the publisher will get to me. And I promise to make every effort to answer them all. (Including a self-addressed envelope would certainly make it easier for me to keep this promise.)

SID SACKSON

Contents

One

In
SEARCH of
BIG and LITTLE
GAME

F OR THIRTY YEARS I have collected games with the single-minded acquisitiveness of the confirmed hobbyist. The popular games are easy to come by and all of them are neatly on my shelves or methodically recorded in an extensive card file.

Of much greater challenge is the forgotten game. Most of these thirty years have been spent in pursuit of such games. My search has led me to libraries, museums, secondhand bookstores, department stores, and out-of-the-way toy shops all over the United States, Canada, and several countries in Europe.

Often at the end of the trail I find that the quarry was hardly worth the chase. But other times there is a prize that makes all the effort worthwhile, a game that, through unfortunate circumstances, was doomed to an untimely death, but one that eminently deserves to be revived.

MATE is certainly such a game. It is a card game played with only twenty cards. Yet with this limited material an amazing diversity of playing situations develop. And it is, almost unique among card games, completely a game of skill.

In Hanover, Germany, in the year 1915, G. Capellen published a small booklet entitled *"Zwei neue Kriegspiele!"* ("Two New War Games!"). One was FREE CHESS, a variant of the board game. The other was MATE. Obviously the time was not right for two make-believe war games while the reality of World War I occupied the center of the stage. So Herr Capellen's booklet never emerged from obscurity. Through the kindly persistence of a bookdealer's wife I obtained a copy. (The only other I have come across is a part of the CHESS collection in the Royal Library at The Hague, the Netherlands.)

This dealer does an extensive mail-order business in books and periodicals on CHESS and CHECKERS. Occasionally, and reluctantly, he gets material on off-beat games which he banishes to an obscure shelf. If he is in a very good mood he will admit me to check the contents of the shelf. Otherwise he will insist that he has nothing, which means that I am dismissed.

I fare much better when his wife is in attendance. One day she pointed out Herr Capellen's booklet. At that time my knowledge of German was limited to the conventional response to a sneeze, so I saw little point in making the purchase. It took her some time, but she finally convinced me that somehow I would manage. Surprisingly, with the aid of a secondhand grammar and dictionary, I found that she was right.

MATE   *by G. Capellen*

● *Number of players.* Two.
● *The deck.* From a standard deck of cards use the following twenty:

♣A	♣10	♣K	♣Q	♣7
♠A	♠10	♠K	♠Q	♠7
♡A	♡10	♡K	♡Q	♡7
◇A	◇10	◇K	◇Q	◇7

This is known as the "Single Mate Deck." The game, at the option of the players, can also be played with the "Double Mate Deck," which is made up from two ordinary decks as follows (the decks should preferably have the same backs):

♣A	♣10	♣K	♣7	♣7
♠A	♠10	♠K	♠K	♠7
♡A	♡10	♡10	♡K	♡7
◇A	◇A	◇10	◇K	◇7

(Until the players are familiar with the game, it is a good idea to copy the above table on a piece of paper, or an index card, and keep it handy for reference.)

In both decks the suits rank in value as shown, with clubs the highest and diamonds the lowest. (This is the same sequence as in CONTRACT BRIDGE except that here clubs are placed at the top rather than at the bottom.) The cards rank in value as shown, with Ace being the highest and 7 the lowest.

● *The play.* One player, whom we will call X, is chosen to deal the first hand. He shuffles the cards and deals ten to each, in groups of five at a time.

X, the dealer, leads any card he wishes. Y, the opponent, must then play a card of the same suit. If he has more than one card of that suit, he may play whichever he chooses. If he lacks a card of the suit led, he must play a card of the same rank (such as Ace on Ace, 10 on 10, etc.). The cards, as they are played, are kept face up in front of each player instead of being played to the center of the table.

The two cards, one from each player, constitute the first "move" (in keeping with the fact that MATE has more in common with board games of skill than with card games, this term is used rather than "trick"). The player who played the higher card, or the higher suit when rank is followed, leads for the second move. When playing with the Double Mate Deck it is possible for two identical cards to be played on a move. In this case the first to be played is considered the higher.

Play continues in this manner until a player leads a card that his opponent cannot follow, either in suit or rank. The player leading the card has given "mate" to his opponent, and play stops. If all ten moves can be played without a mate, it is a "draw."

● *Scoring.* For purposes of scoring a mate, each card is considered to have a value as follows: Ace = 11, 10 = 10, King = 4, Queen = 3, 7 = 7. The value of the mating card is multiplied by the number of the move in which the mate is given. For example, if a player gives mate with a Queen in the first move he scores $3 \times 1 = 3$ points, while if he gives mate with an Ace in the tenth move, he scores $11 \times 10 = 110$ points.

In case of a draw neither player scores.

● *Rounds and Matches.* After the first game has been played and scored, the cards are picked up and, without being reshuffled, exchanged between the players. Y, who now has the cards X previously held, leads any card he wishes to start the second game. Two games constitute a "round" and, since each player has the opportunity to play each hand, the luck of the deal is eliminated.

After the first round, Y gathers the cards, shuffles them, and deals out new hands. A second round is now played in a similar manner to the first. Two rounds constitute a "match." The player who has scored the greater total number of points is the winner of the match and the measure of his victory is the difference between the two total scores.

● *Foreplacing and Overmate.* "Foreplacing" of cards is an important

4

part of the game, but I have postponed introducing it until the beginner has had a chance to familiarize himself with the basic play. Advanced players can make use of foreplacing to reap the largest possible score from a particular hand.

Foreplacing allows the players, at the start of each individual game, to remove a card from their hand, show it, and then place it face down before them. A foreplaced card does not enter into the play of that game. The contestant who will lead to the first move announces whether he wishes to foreplace a card, after which the opponent has a similar choice. The opponent, however, may not foreplace a card of the same suit or rank as that foreplaced by the first player.

If a player who foreplaces a card succeeds in giving mate, the multiplying number of the move is increased by 1. Thus, in this case, a mate given in the seventh move with a King scores $8 \times 4 = 32$ points.

If both players foreplace a card there will be a maximum of only nine moves in the game. If only one player foreplaces a card, and the game proceeds that far, the player with only nine cards uses his ninth played card also as his tenth. A mate given in this tenth move is known as an "overmate" and scores double. Thus, an overmate given with an Ace scores $11 \times 11 \times 2 = 242$ points (the maximum possible) for the player who foreplaced. The other player would score $10 \times 11 \times 2 = 220$ points.

● *Variations.* The following rules can be added to the basic game for a change of pace. The particular variation to be used must, of course, be agreed on in advance by the players.

1. *Mate with Free Move.* Once during an individual game either player X or player Y (whoever uses it first) may, even though he has a card of the same suit as that led, answer the lead with a card of the same rank, announcing "Free move" as he does so.

2. *Mate with King's Privilege.* When a King is led the opponent must follow with another King if he has one. If not, he follows with a card of the same suit.

   Figure Privilege is the same as King's Privilege except that the same rule applies to Queens as well as Kings.

3. *Mate with Free Move and King's (or Figure) Privilege.* This is a combination of variation 1 and variation 2. If the Free Move is taken in answer to the play of a King (or Queen), it allows the player to follow in suit even though he has another King (or Queen) which he could play.

● *Samples of play.* These sample games are taken from the original book and illustrate the different ways in which a strong hand can be played to obtain the highest score. The underlined card in each move is the card that was led.

The Single Mate Deck is used and is dealt out as follows:

	X			Y	
♣	A, 10, K		♣		Q, 7
♠	A, 10, K, Q		♠		7
♡	A, Q, 7		♡	10, K,	
◇	—		◇	A, 10, K, Q, 7	

First game:

Move	X	Y
Foreplaced	♠K	—
1.	♡Q	♡K
2.	♣A	◇A
3.	♠Q	♠7
4.	♠10	♡10
5.	♣10	♣Q
6.	♣K	♣7
7.	♡7	◇7
8.	♠A	—

X wins 9 × 11 = 99 points.

Second game (*with hands reversed*):

Move	Y	X
Foreplaced	♠K	—
1.	♣K	♣Q
2.	♣A	♣7
3.	♣10	◇10
4.	♠Q	♠7
5.	♠10	♡10
6.	♡A	♡K
7.	♡Q	◇Q
8.	♡7	◇7
9.	♠A	◇A
10.	(♠A)	—

(Y chooses to foreplace the same card that X chose. He could have foreplaced another card, or none at all.)

Y wins 11 × 11 × 2 = 242 points (Maximum Mate).

The same hands played with Figure Privilege:

Move	X	Y	
Foreplaced	♡7	—	
1.	♡A	♡K	
2.	♠K	◇K	(King's Privilege)
3.	♣K	♣7	
4.	♣A	♣Q	
5.	♣10	◇10	
6.	♡Q	◇Q	(Queen's Privilege)
7.	♠Q	♠7	
8.	♠10	♡10	
9.	♠A	◇A	
10.	(♠A)	—	

X wins $11 \times 11 \times 2 = 242$ points (Maximum Mate).

No. 748,626.

PATENTED JAN. 5, 1904.

L. J. MAGIE.
GAME BOARD.
APPLICATION FILED MAR. 23, 1903.

NO MODEL.

2 SHEETS—SHEET 1.

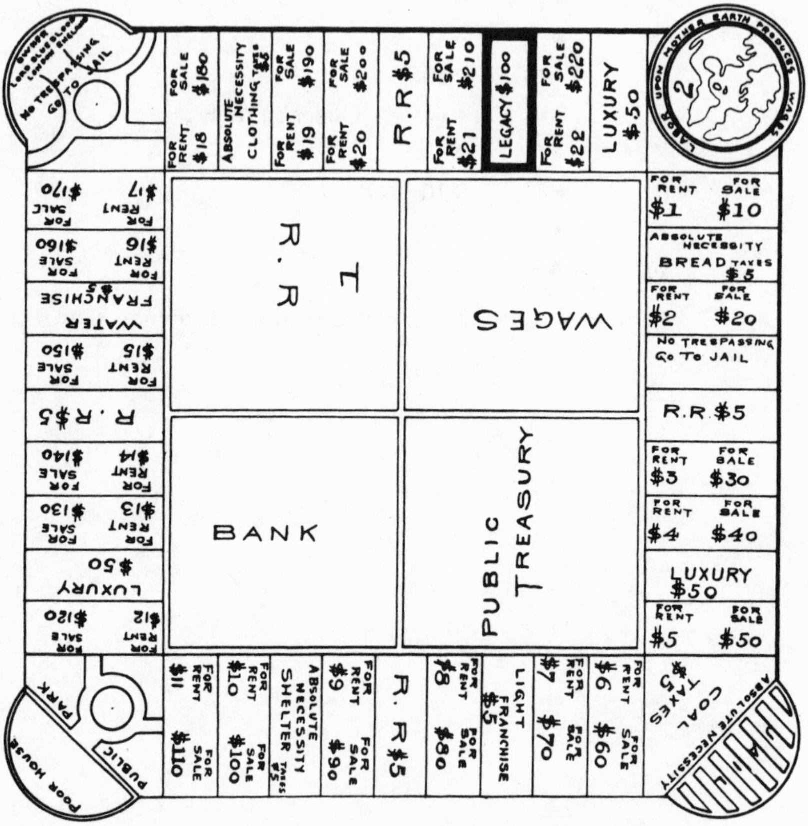

GO TO JAIL
NO TRESPASSING
THE EARTH IS THE LORD'S AND THE FULLNESS THEREOF

LABOR UPON MOTHER EARTH PRODUCES WAGES

FOR RENT $18 / FOR SALE $180	ABSOLUTE NECESSITY CLOTHING Taxes $5	FOR RENT $19 / FOR SALE $190	FOR RENT $20 / FOR SALE $200	R.R. $5	FOR RENT $21 / FOR SALE $210	LEGACY $100	FOR RENT $22 / FOR SALE $220	LUXURY $50

FOR SALE $170 / FOR RENT $17 — FOR RENT $1 / FOR SALE $10

R.R.

FOR RENT $16 / FOR SALE $160 — ABSOLUTE NECESSITY BREAD Taxes $5

FRANCHISE WATER $5 — FOR RENT $2 / FOR SALE $20

FOR SALE $150 / FOR RENT $15 — NO TRESPASSING GO TO JAIL

WAGES

R.R. $5 — R.R. $5

FOR SALE $140 / FOR RENT $14 — FOR RENT $3 / FOR SALE $30

FOR SALE $130 / FOR RENT $13 — FOR RENT $4 / FOR SALE $40

BANK

PUBLIC TREASURY

LUXURY $50 — LUXURY $50

FOR SALE $120 / FOR RENT $12 — FOR RENT $5 / FOR SALE $50

| FOR RENT $11 / FOR SALE $110 | FOR RENT $10 / FOR SALE $100 | ABSOLUTE NECESSITY SHELTER Taxes $5 / FOR RENT $9 / FOR SALE $90 | R.R. $5 | FOR RENT $8 / FOR SALE $80 | LIGHT FRANCHISE $5 | FOR RENT $7 / FOR SALE $70 | FOR RENT $6 / FOR SALE $60 | COAL TAXES $5 | ABSOLUTE NECESSITY |

PARK
PUBLIC
POOR HOUSE

Fig. 1.

Witnesses
F. L. Ourand.
M. H. Ourand.

Inventor
Lizzie J. Magie
by John A. Saul
Attorney

THE FILES OF PATENTS that have been granted are a fruitful hunting ground for forgotten games, although going through these files, as anyone who has ever been involved in a patent search well knows, is a time consuming job. Often the patented games are downright silly, such as a set of dominos made of rubber so that they can double as ink erasers (No. 729,489) or a sliding block puzzle with edible pieces so that a player who despairs of a solution can find consolation in gratifying his stomach (No. 1,274,294). Often the patents are repetitious: There are over a hundred variations of the well-known checkerboard and over a thousand different baseball games.

But often the patented games are a fascinating reflection of their time: races to the North Pole, war games to capture the Kaiser, automobile games, in the infancy of the automobile, and radio games for the crystal-set fanatic.

On January 5, 1904, Patent No. 748,626 was granted to Lizzie J. Magie for a game board. The game, known as THE LANDLORD'S GAME, was based on the then current "single-tax" theory of economist Henry George.

The board, reproduced here from the original patent, is undoubtedly recognizable to anyone who has ever played MONOPOLY, and is there anyone who hasn't? In the 1930s Charles Darrow, an unemployed heating engineer, added the concept of building houses on the rental property, after obtaining a monopoly of all properties of the same color.° He thereby created the most popular proprietary board game of all time and ended up a millionaire.

Preceding THE LANDLORD'S GAME by just under a year, on April 21, 1903, Patent No. 726,023 was granted to Henry Busch and Arthur Jaeger, also for a game board. Their game, called BLUE AND GRAY, made no lasting impression in the world of games which, I suppose, is understandable since it didn't have the innovative qualities of THE LANDLORD'S GAME. Yet it was, and is, a delightful pastime, which should particularly appeal to the CHECKERS fan who is looking for something different.

The name BLUE AND GRAY, of course, refers to the uniforms of the South and the North in the Civil War and in the original game the playing pieces of the contestants were of those colors.

° I have since been informed that in the early 1920s a game—already named MONOPOLY—was being played in a number of east coast college towns. The sets were home made and usually gave local names to the "properties," but all the features of the final game were present.

BLUE AND GRAY   *by Henry Busch and Arthur Jaeger*

• *Number of players.* Two.

• *Equipment.* A playing board as shown. This can be quickly sketched in pencil on a large sheet of paper or, once addicted to the game, you can create a more permanent board on cardboard by using india ink. I doctored a checkerboard by pasting a sheet of colored paper over the four center squares and then putting in the heavy line with thin strips of an adhesive cloth (such as mystic tape) in a contrasting color. In cutting the strips, about 3/16″ wide, it doesn't matter if the cut is not too neat. In fact a certain amount of irregularity makes the final appearance more attractive. The whole project took me less than an hour.

Each contestant has eighteen pieces, one captain (marked in the diagram with a C) and seventeen guards. The pieces are set up, as shown, in the two front rows, using the intersection of the lines rather than the centers of the squares. For pieces, two sets of checkers can be used or, better still, small (7/8″ diameter) poker chips. The captain can be designated by two piled pieces or by a distinguishing mark pasted onto a single piece.

• *The play.* Each player in turn moves either his captain or one of his guards.

The captain moves one position forward (toward the star in the center of the board) along the heavy line. If the next position along the heavy line is occupied, the captain cannot move until it is vacated.

Guards move one position in any direction along any line, including a diagonal. Guards, however, may not enter the area in the center of the board.

• *Capturing.* Guards capture opposing guards by jumping, as in CHECKERS. The jumping guard and the captured guard must be next to each other along a line, and the adjacent position along the same straight line must be vacant. Again as in CHECKERS, multiple jumps can be made if the guards to be captured are in proper position.

If, in a player's turn, he has a guard in position to make a jump, he must do so and must continue jumping as long as that guard is in a position to jump. If more than one guard is able to jump, the player is free to choose the one he will use.

Captains can neither jump nor be jumped.

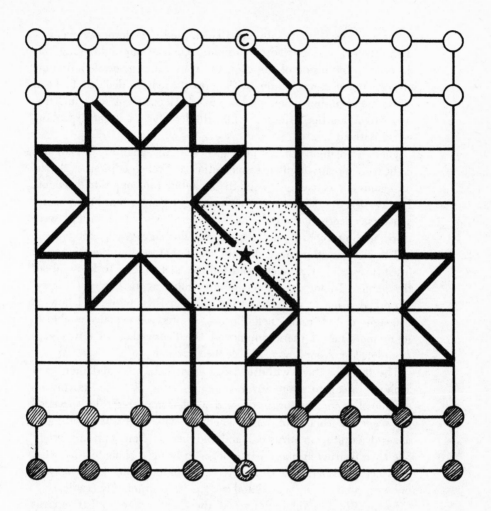

● *Winning the game.* The player who moves his captain onto the star in the center of the board is the winner.

If both captains are blocked by opposing guards and neither player is able to break the impasse the game is won by the player whose captain is farther advanced along the heavy line. In playing a series of games, it is my practice to count a game won in this manner as half a game.

SEVERAL YEARS AGO my wife and I celebrated a wedding anniversary with a trip to Europe. To her despair, much of our sightseeing was devoted to the inside of libraries, toy stores, and game departments of department stores. Later in the trip she wisely decided to head off on her own, but when we hit our first department store in Paris, Aux Trois Quartiers, she was still afraid to face a French-speaking world without me.

There were more than thirty games at the counter and all but eight were already familiar to me, either as French editions of American games or as having crossed the Atlantic in the opposite direction. I proceeded to read the rules of these eight games, that being, as far as I was concerned, the only way of determining which, if any, were worth adding to our potentially overweight baggage.

The clerk in attendance did not see it that way and continued to insist, in French, that she would tell me all I needed to know about the games. Taking advantage of my status as an ignorant tourist, I pretended not to understand her and persisted with my labors. A colleague called from a neighboring counter was equally unable to deter me. One of them summoned the floorwalker who was at a complete loss about how to handle the situation.

The three of them withdrew, conferred earnestly, and then used a phone to call for help. Several minutes later, as I was starting on the fourth game, a smartly dressed woman appeared. She surveyed the scene for a moment, approached my wife who was standing to one side, quite embarrassed, and bid her a "Bon jour, madame." She then instructed one on the clerks to bring a chair for my wife. This accomplished, she withdrew with another "Bon jour," leaving my wife comfortably seated and me free to continue my studies.

Eventually I purchased two of the games. One, called PETITES ANNONCES DE FRANCE-SOIR (which translates as Classified Ads of *France-Soir* [a popular evening newspaper]), has a delightful gallic flavor. Players move around a board showing a map of Paris. They acquire children by landing on the proper spaces. The children are educated by landing on other spaces, after which they are sent out to work. The winner is the first player who is able, by using the earnings of his children, to buy a bank.

The problem of transporting all the games picked up during the trip developed into a serious one. To save room a trail of discarded boxes was left in our hotel wastebaskets and the game equipment packed tighter and tighter into the surviving boxes. At the end of the trip there were five boxes containing the contents of eighteen games.

On the last day we closed the valises with great difficulty, had them weighed in at the London air terminal and, with four hours to kill, set off on another shopping expedition. Our fifteen-year-old daughter, who beat us to London by one month, had requested us to buy her a particular miniskirt in a Chelsea boutique.

We located the boutique but, unfortunately, not the desired skirt. Close to the boutique was a large toy store which I couldn't resist. In it I bought the game of White Knights, a small game which was placed in a small bag. Then, as an afterthought, I purchased a set of Cuisenaire Counting Sticks which came with a bag large enough to hold my original purchase. In another toy store I bought the game of Oil and finally, in Peter Jones department store, the game of Combat. Each succeeding bag was large enough to hold the preceding one.

Our customs inspector, a somewhat larger edition of Alan Sherman, had evidently never run across a game collector before. The five boxes with the equipment for eighteen games troubled him. Long after our fellow passengers were homeward bound he was still poking around in our valises. Tiring of this, he turned to the large bag I was carrying.

"What's in there?" he asked.

"Games," I answered.

He wanted to see for himself. Each time I withdrew a game and another bag he became more curious about the contents of the new bag. Finally we arrived at the game of White Knights.

"Open it!" he demanded. I did, exposing a folding board sitting upon a cardboard platform.

"What's under there?"

"Nothing—I hope." By this time his suspicion had become contagious and my hand trembled as I removed the platform. My heart started beating again when I saw that there were no diamonds or dope cached below.

"Welcome home," he said.

Backtracking to London, a good part of my stay there was spent in the British Museum, but the only part I ever saw was the reading room. For anyone who is intending to make use of this magnificent reference facility, it is important to know that, since space is extremely limited, a pass is required. Arranging for this in advance, as I did, can save considerable time.

Many irreplaceable books on games were destroyed in the German bombing during World War II, but a wealth of information remains. In a delightful 1912 French book by E. Lanes, entitled *Nouveau Manuel Complet des Jeux de Cartes* (*New Complete Manual of Card Games*), I found the following game of LE TRUC which, to the best of my knowledge, translates as THE KNACK.

LE TRUC is a fast-moving game with much of the flavor of POKER, but it is definitely interesting enough to be played by two players, and without money.

The rules, as is so often the case in old game books, are not too well organized and in some points are unclear. For readers who would like to make their own interpretations rather than being bound by mine, I will present an exact translation of the original. Where I feel they may help, I'll insert parenthetical remarks and at the end I'll include further clarifications and also some variations I have used to add new flavor to the game.

LE TRUC   *Anon.*

LE TRUC is a very lively and pleasant game; it is played a great deal in the south (of France). It is above all a game of bluff, which is why it is sometimes called the little French POKER.

It is played by two or four players, with a deck of thirty-two cards (the traditional French PIQUET deck, consisting of the Ace down to the 7 in the four suits).

Cards are drawn to choose a dealer. The dealer shuffles the cards, has them cut and distributes them, one by one, until each player has three cards.

The highest card is the 7, followed by the 8—called 6, probably because it is worth less than the 7; in this description we will call it by its true name: 8. Then in decreasing order comes Ace, King, Queen, Jack, 10, and 9, which is the lowest card.

In certain localities, the Ace replaces the 8; in that case the decreasing order of the cards is: 7, Ace, King, Queen, Jack, 10, 9, and 8. We will explain the game with 8 as the second highest card.

Let us start with the game for two.

In LE TRUC suit has no bearing, that is to say, any King will take a Queen of the same suit or of another suit.

The game is usually played to 12 points and in rubbers (which means, for those not familiar with the term from BRIDGE, that the first to win two 12-point games is the winner), because if not played in rubbers, often the contest will be over in the first hand.

The cards having been dealt, the pone (nondealer) can, if he is not satisfied with his hand, ask for new cards; if the dealer accepts (if not, the hands are played as dealt), the hands are discarded without being shown and three new cards are dealt to each, one by one as before, without the deck being reshuffled and recut. If the pone wishes to play, he throws a card on the table, usually his highest card, because it is very advantageous to take the first trick. In order to win, it is necessary to take two tricks out of three; if one of the tricks is spoiled, it is the first taken of the other two that wins the hand. A trick is said to be spoiled when the opponent plays a card of the same rank as the card led. Thus, if on a 7 the opponent plays another 7, the trick is spoiled.

One sees how important it is to take the first trick, since the one who takes it wins if the second or third trick is spoiled.

If the pone throws a card on the table, the dealer, before placing his card, can say "Two points if I play," which means the hand will be played for 2 points instead of 1. If the pone accepts, he says "Play"; but if he refuses, he throws his cards face down on the table and the dealer scores 1 point.

If the dealer plays to the trick, he either takes it, leaves it for the pone, or spoils it. The winner of a trick, or in the case of a spoiled trick, the one who led to it, leads to the next trick. Whoever leads to the second trick may simply play or may propose "Two more if I play," which means the hand will be played for 4 points instead of 2. If the other player refuses, the proposing player scores 2 points.

The hand continues in this way with each contestant at his turn to play having the right to propose an increase in the stakes, up to a proposal of "my remainder." That means he proposes to play for all the points he is short of 12 at that time.

But if the other player needs more points to reach 12, he may, at his turn, propose "my remainder" (he certainly has nothing to lose by doing so) and whoever wins the hand wins the game.

It has been stated that there is much bluffing in this game; in effect, it often happens that a player having only a poor hand proposes a large increase in the stakes in order to scare off his adversary, and, if successful, scores all the points that were proposed and accepted prior to his last proposition.

Suppose that the pone has an exceptionally good hand; for example two 7s and an 8. If the hand is played simply, he gains and scores only 1 point. In this case, in order to fool his adversary, who may have a good or moderately good hand, it is necessary (if you have the nerve) to pretend not to have anything worthwhile and to ask for new cards. If the dealer refuses, the pone plays his eight, so as not to show the beauty of his hand at once, and if the dealer has, for example, a 7 and an 8 he will play the 7 and propose 2 or 4 points. The pone will accept and then raise the stakes with a proposition of "my remainder." If the dealer takes this as a bluff, he will accept and lead his 8 and the pone will take the last two tricks with his two 7s.

When four play, the cards are cut to form two partnerships (the two high cards and the two low cards each being paired). The partners are seated face to face, separated on the right and on the left by their adversaries.

In each of the two partnerships, one player conducts the play of the hand (by telling his partner to play his highest, his lowest, etc.) and his partner indicates to him, by conventional signs, the strong cards that he possesses. For example, a grin (appropriately) indicates a 7; the same sign repeated, two 7s; a wink, an 8; a shrug, an Ace. It is just about certain that these signs are seen and understood by the adversaries; but the hand of the partner who conducts the play is not indicated and, since only twelve out of thirty-two cards are distributed, its value remains a mystery to the adversary.

As with two players, tricks are spoiled when, with the four cards played, the highest card of one side is covered by an equally high card from the other side. In this case the one who led to the spoiled trick leads to the next.

As with two players, the side winning the first trick is the winner if one of the other two is spoiled.

If all three tricks are spoiled—when played by two or by four—the hand is void and the deal passes to the next dealer.

IT IS NOT CLEAR whether, in a two-hand game, the pone can ask for new cards just once or whether he can do so repeatedly, as long as the dealer accepts and the deck holds out. My experience has been that a better game results when only one new hand is allowed.

It is, again, not clear whether new cards can be requested in the four-hand game or not. My practice is not to use this feature when playing with four. I also find the four-hand game more interesting when each player handles his own game rather than having one partner take over for the team.

While the rules seem to indicate that the dealer's only allowable proposal before playing to the first trick is "Two points if I play," and the leader to the second trick is limited to a proposal of "Two more if I play," the example given later shows the players in these positions free to propose a greater increase. The author's probable intent is to allow any augmentation of the stakes that a player, at his turn, wishes to propose.

LE TRUC, like POKER, is a basic idea which lends itself to many variations. The following are three variations for two players which I, with the help of my wife, derived. I am sure that the interested reader will be able to come up with many more.

In the variations the general rules hold unless specifically changed.

1. The pone may make one request for a new hand, which may be accepted or refused by the dealer.

    Each player before each play of a card, including the lead to the first trick, can propose a double by saying "Double to 2," "Double to 4," "Double to 8," etc. If all possible doubles are made and accepted, there will be six, which would make the value of the hand 64 points.

    Game is 16 points, but the actual payoff value to the winner of a game can be greater or lesser as follows. From the winner's final score which, due to doubles in the last hand, can be 16 or more points, deduct 1 point for each hand that has been played (as counted on the scoresheet). Thus if a player's final score is 19 and a total of eleven hands have been played, his payoff is 8 points. (This scoring keeps a player with a good lead from playing it safe and avoiding doubles, since each hand played deducts 1 point from his final payoff.)

2. This is the same as variation 1 except that it is played with each player holding five cards, which allows for more play and more doubling.

3. Each player is dealt five cards. The pone, without the necessity of asking permission of the dealer, may discard as many cards as he wishes and replace them from the deck. The dealer then has the same privilege. Play of the game and scoring are the same as in the previous variations.

    Since both players are apt to get better hands, in this variation the doubling can get pretty wild. The contestants may agree to set game at a higher total, such as 24 points or even 32.

THERE HAS ALWAYS BEEN an interest in books that instruct those fortunate enough to have leisure on how to fill it. As early as 1551 a
book dedicated to Catherine de Medici and describing one hundred
games was published in Bologna. In my collection I have a copy
of the third edition of this book, *Cento Giuochi Liberali, et D'Ingegno,*
dated 1580. Judging by its ready availability some four hundred years
later, it must have been a best seller.

While, since 1551, there has been a steady flow of such books from
many countries, toward the end of the last century in the United
States and England it developed into a flood. One of the biggest, and
in many ways one of the best, of these was a 784-page volume published in 1890 in the United States entitled *The Young Folks' Cy-
clopaedia of Games and Sports* by John D. Champlin and Arthur
E. Bostwick.

From A-B-C, a card game, to Zoetrope, a coming attraction for the
moving picture, it is jam-packed with games, pastimes, sports, and
scientific experiments. One particularly interesting game is PLANK,
which undoubtedly was a proprietary game of its time but has since
completely disappeared. PLANK is interesting because it takes the
trivial game of TIC-TAC-TOE and, by adding color and movement,
gives it a new scope and dimension.

You will need special equipment to play PLANK, but it is simple
to prepare and a workable set can be readied within an hour.

PLANK   *Anon.*

- *Number of players.* Two, three, or four.
- *Equipment.* Twelve "planks," which are cardboard strips divided
into three square boxes. The three boxes are colored red, white, and
blue in one of the patterns shown, there being four of each pattern.

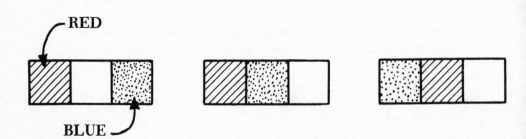

(If the squares are made 1½" on a side, two planks can be cut from a 3" × 5" index card, with a half inch of waste.)

Twenty-four markers. These come in four sets of six markers each, the sets being identified by the letters A, B, C, and D. In each set of six, two of the markers are red, two are white, and two are blue.

(These can be cut from colored cardboard, about 1" square being a good size; or they can be made by pasting letters onto poker chips.)

● *The game for two.* Take one marker from the A set and one from the B. Place them face down, mix them, and have each player draw one. The players take the remaining markers of their set and the one with A will begin the play. If a series of games is played, keep the same markers and alternate playing first.

Shuffle the twelve planks and deal them out so that each player has six. These are placed face up on the table in front of the players.

● *The play.* The beginning player lays one of his planks in the center of the table and places a marker on the square of the same color. His opponent may then either place a marker on the same plank or lay another plank next to the original, long sides touching, and place a marker on the new plank. The play continues in this manner with each player in turn either placing a marker on one of the previously laid planks or putting down a new plank and placing a marker on it.

After all six of a player's markers have been placed, he, in subsequent turns, moves any one of his markers to a new position, either on a plank already laid or on a new one.

After all of a player's planks have been laid, he is limited to placing his markers on planks already down.

Remember: Markers must always be placed in squares of the same color as the marker; if a player lays down a new plank he must in that turn place a marker on it; planks are always placed with long sides touching.

● *Winning the game.* The first player to get three of his markers, red, white, and blue—but not necessarily in that order—in a continuous straight line is the winner. The line may be across one plank or lengthwise over three planks, but it may not be diagonal.

● *Sample game.* The planks dealt to each of the players are shown on the sides. In the center the entire game is shown, the sequence of plays being indicated by numbers. It will be a lot easier to follow if the game pieces are used to set up the game step by step.

1. *A* starts the game by laying down a plank with a blue center, since he has three of them, and placing a blue marker in the square of that color.

2. *B* must stop *A* from getting two markers in a row lengthwise with both ends open, or the game will be over practically before it starts. The plank used stops *A* in one direction and placing a red marker gives *B* a free line to work on. He, however, uses his only plank with a blue center.

3. *A* threatens to complete a line.

4. *B* answers *A*'s threat by again using the plank to do the blocking and places a blue marker in a free line.

5. *A* does not lay a plank. Instead he places a red marker which threatens completion of a line and at the same time blocks *B* off in one direction.

6. *B* must defend against the threat.

7. *A* is pretty well stopped. This is an attempt to open up new territory.

8. *B* poses a double threat.

9. *A* places his marker in the red square, since both of *B*'s blue markers have already been placed.

10. *B* answers *A*'s threat. He also opens up another potential threat which will come into play as soon as all the markers are placed and moving to new positions begins.

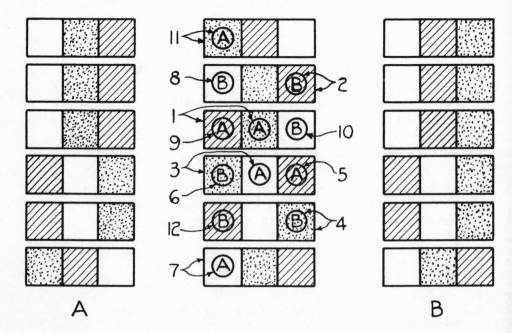

A   B

11. *A* blocks this potential threat by using a plank. He places his last marker in the blue square.

12. *B* places his last marker in position to pose another threat. *A* can now move a blue marker to stop the upper threat or a white marker to stop the lower threat, but he cannot stop both. *B* wins.

● *The game for three.* Take a marker from the *A*, *B*, and *C* sets, and have each player draw one. The player with *A* will play first. The player with *B* is seated to *A*'s left and will play second, etc. In subsequent games the same markers are kept and first play rotates to the left.

The planks are dealt out so that each player has four.

The rules of play are the same as in the game for two.

In any game of strategy where three players compete individually, a situation can arise where one player has to be stopped and each of the other players can stop him, but at some expense to their own game. To provide an incentive in this situation, I have introduced the following scoring system (which is not a part of the game as originally published).

When a player wins a game, the player to his left has 2 points scored against him while the third player is penalized only 1. At the end of the agreed number of games, the player with the lowest score is the winner. This method of scoring puts the burden of stopping a player upon the one immediately following.

● *The game for four.* Take a marker from all of the sets and have each player draw one. Seat the players so that they are arranged in clockwise sequence from *A* to *D*. *A* and *C* will be partners against *B* and *D*. *A* plays first. In subsequent games the same markers are kept and first play rotates to the left.

The planks are dealt out so that each player has three.

The rules of play are the same as in the game for two.

Each player uses his own markers and planks and cannot play those of his partner. A team wins when either member completes a winning line. A winning line may not consist of markers of both partners in combination.

Before starting, the contestants should determine whether partners will be allowed to suggest plays to each other, particularly in case of a threat from the opponents, or whether this will be prohibited. With beginners it is usually preferable to allow consultation, while with more advanced players it makes for a much better game if each partner must watch out for himself.

DURING THE PROLIFIC LATTER HALF of the nineteenth century a great many card games were introduced in Europe and the United States; to mention a few: BEZIQUE, FEMME SOLE, NOBLESSE OBLIGE, NORSEMAN, PINOCHLE, TENS, VETO, and ZETEMA. Of these BEZIQUE achieved a lasting popularity in Europe; PINOCHLE, of course, remains an American favorite; and the others have long since been forgotten.

It is impossible to know why some games make it and others don't. By all standards of merit the last game on my little list, ZETEMA, should have been accepted, yet as early as 1876, when the book *Cards and Card Tricks* by H. E. Heather was published in England, the author had this to say: "ZETEMA is pronounced, and justly so, by most players, to be far superior to BEZIQUE. This game, however, does not appear to initiate itself in public favour as its merits deserve. It was introduced a few years ago by Messrs. Joseph Hunt & Sons, and issued by them with special markers, cards, and rules, like its more popular rival."

ZETEMA is unique in its objectives of play, belonging to neither the RUMMY nor the trick-taking family of games; although the term "trick" is used in a different context. Good judgment, rather than brain-busting analysis, is required to play well, which makes ZETEMA a relaxing, but fascinating, evening's pastime. And, incidentally, the special markers and cards furnished by Messrs. Hunt & Sons are not at all necessary.

ZETEMA   *Anon.*

● *Number of players.* Two, three, four, or six.
● *The deck.* A sixty-five-card deck made up by adding to one fifty-two-card deck a full suit from a second. It doesn't matter which suit is chosen as long as the players are informed as to its identity.
● *Definitions.* The following are special terms used in the game.

An *assembly* is the holding of five cards of the same rank in hand at the same time (such as five Aces, or five Kings, etc.).

A *flush* is all six cards in a hand being of the same suit, except that the duplicated suit, having double the number of cards, cannot be used for forming a flush.

A *sequence* consists of all six cards in hand running in numerical order, suit not being considered. The Ace can be used either as high

(A, K, Q, J, 10, and 9) or as low (6, 5, 4, 3, 2, and A) but not in an around-the-corner sequence (such as 2, A, K, Q, J, and 10).

A *marriage* is a King and Queen of the same suit. A marriage is declared by playing the two cards from the hand at one time or, if either card has already been played to the table, adding the matching card to it.

An *imperial marriage* is the second marriage in the duplicated suit.

A *trick* is five cards of the same rank played onto the table. The player adding the fifth card scores for the trick.

● *Scoring table.* Scores can be obtained in several ways (as will be explained later), and the following is a listing of all the possible scores. (Where two values are given for a particular classification, the unbracketed value is the original one, while the figure in brackets is mine and represents, I believe, an improved scoring. Assemblies are most difficult to make and even at the increased value are rarely worth trying for. Sequences are comparatively easy to complete and tend to dominate the play if valued at 30 points.)

Assemblies

Kings or Queens	100	[130]
Jacks	90	[120]
Aces or 5s	80	[110]
Any other card	60	[100]

Marriages

One marriage	10
Imperial marriage	20
Two marriages at one time	30
Two marriages at one time, one being imperial	40
Two marriages of the same suit at one time	50
Three marriages at one time	60
Three marriages at one time, one being imperial	70
Three marriages at one time, two being of the duplicated suit	80
Four marriages at one time	100
Four marriages at one time, one being imperial	110
Four marriages at one time, two being of the duplicated suit	120
Five marriages at one time	150

Flushes and Sequences

Flush ————————————————————	30	
Sequence ———————————————————	30	[20]
Flush and Sequence ——————————————		[50]

(This possibility is not covered in the original rules.)

Tricks

Kings or Queens—when made ————————————	50
Jacks —————————————————————	20
Aces or 5s —————————————————	15
Any other card ———————————————	5

● *Preliminary.* When two or three play, each scores his own game. When four or six play, cut cards to determine two sets of partners and seat the players so that the teams alternate.

Cut for dealer, low card receiving the nod. In subsequent hands the deal rotates to the left.

If two, three, or four are playing, deal six cards to each. If six are playing, deal only five cards to each. (In this case a flush or sequence consists of only five cards, but scores the same number of points.)

The remainder of the deck is placed face down in the center of the table where all players can reach it.

● *The play.* Starting with eldest hand (the player on the dealer's left, who was dealt to first), each player in turn makes one of the following plays:

1. Place a card face up in the center of the table. Each rank is placed in a separate pile and a new card of the same rank is put on top, but overlapping so that the number of cards in the pile is apparent.

   If the player places the fifth card on a pile he has completed a trick and scores it at once. The cards of the trick are turned over and placed aside.

   The player completes his turn by drawing a card from the top of the deck, bringing his hand back to six cards.

2. Declare a flush, or sequence, or a combination of both. The player shows the combination to the other players and scores it.

   The player keeps his hand, however, except for one card which he places in the same way as in (1). He may, if able, score for a trick (making it possible to score twice in one turn).

He completes his turn by drawing a card from the deck. (The new card may fill out another combination which can be declared in the next turn.)

3. Declare one or more marriages. For each marriage, the player uses either two cards from his hand or one card from his hand matching a card that has been placed on the table.

   The marriage or marriages are scored and all the cards used are turned over and placed aside. The player draws enough cards from the deck to bring his hand to six cards again, which completes his turn.

   (As an example let us suppose that hearts are the duplicated suit and that the following Kings and Queens have been placed on the table: ♡K, ♣K, ◇Q. The player has ♡K, ♡Q, ♡Q, ◇K in his hand. He plays the four cards from his hand, takes the ♡K and ◇Q from the table, and makes three marriages, two in hearts and one in diamonds. From the scoring table we see that he receives 80 points.)

   Once a marriage has been declared it becomes impossible for a King or Queen trick to be completed in that hand.

4. Declare an assembly. The player removes the five cards from his hand, scores them, and places them aside. He completes his turn by drawing five cards from the deck.

● *When the deck is exhausted.* Play continues in the same way (except, of course, that cards played from the hand are not replaced) until all the cards have been played. It is possible for one player, because of marriages or an assembly made after the deck is exhausted, to run out of cards before the others do. In this case his turn is skipped as the others play out their cards.

At the end of the hand every card will have been used, either in a trick, assembly, or marriage.

● *Special rule for two players.* When, during the play of the cards after the deck is exhausted, a player completes a trick he is required to continue by playing another card.

● *Winning the game.* When two or three play, 300 points are game. When four or six play, 200 points are game. More than one hand will usually be required to reach this. As soon as a player, or team, reaches a winning score the game is over, the remainder of the hand not being played out.

EVER SINCE THEIR INTRODUCTION into Europe some five hundred years ago, playing cards have been popular with large segments of the population and, through most of this time, have been equally unpopular with others. To circumvent this objection to "The Devil's Picture-Books" many "new and moral" decks have been offered to a public in search of "innocent amusement."

"Yankee Notion Cards" were one such deck published around 1857 in, of course, the United States. The publisher introduced his product with the following statement:

> Believing that a settled prejudice exists with a large class of the community against the old-fashioned cards, the publisher has issued an entirely new style, to the introduction of which into every family circle there cannot possibly be the least objection.
>
> These cards and the games adapted to them, are calculated to discipline and exercise the mind; imparting the utmost quickness and facility in the calculation and combination of figures; accomplishing, under the charm of amusement, the objects sought in the study of mathematics—namely, the strengthening of the mind, and the improvement of the memory.
>
> The new cards have been spoken of by the New York Commercial Advertiser in the following language: "We are glad to see something in the way of domestic games, and social amusement, that we can recommend, not only for its scientific and instructive character, but for its good moral influence."
>
> The publisher, being determined that these cards shall be within the reach of all classes, has fixed the standard price at twenty-five cents per pack.

Sixteen games to be played with the new deck are then described. Many are variations of existing games, fitting them to the new deck. And two, QUIEN SABE and BLACK JOKE, are outright gambling games!

At least one of the new games, however, does live up to the promise of the publisher's message. HEKATON is a mathematical game that makes use of cards as digits and is quite helpful in developing number concepts. It is an excellent family game; interesting for adults and yet one in which the children can often outdo their elders.

Before getting to HEKATON (which can also be played with regular cards) let me give a brief description of the "Yankee Notion Cards."

The deck consists of fifty cards which are divided into five suits—Faces, Flags, Eagles, Stars, and Shields. Each suit contains ten cards numbered from zero to 9. The suit of Faces consists of the following (the other four suits being plain):

1 is Mrs. Sally Smith, John's wife.
2 is the Baby.
3 is an Old Maid.
4 is an Old Bachelor.
5 is "Sweet Seventeen," ready for an offer.
6 is the Parson, also ready for duty.
7 is Ruth, the Quakeress.
8 is Ezekiel, Ruth's husband.
9 is the Watchman.
0 is the original John Smith. The only correct likeness ever taken.

HEKATON   *Anon.*

- *Number of players.* Two or four.
- *The deck.* A deck of fifty cards made up of five each of the following cards. Ace (which is used as a 1), 2, 3, 4, 5, 6, 7, 8, 9, King (which is used as a 0). The cards can be taken from a double deck of standard cards, suit not making any difference.
- *The game for four.* Cut cards to choose two teams and seat the partners across from each other. The player with the lowest card deals first and distributes twelve cards to each player, the two remaining cards being placed face up on the table. In subsequent hands the deal rotates to the left.
- *The play.* The player to the dealer's left starts by playing a card to the table, completing a trick if able. Play continues in a clockwise direction, each contestant playing one card in turn, completing tricks when able, until all the cards in hand have been played.
- *Tricks.* A trick consists of a number of cards arranged on the table either to form, or add up to, a number that is a multiple of 100. The resultant number is credited to the score of the player making the trick.

The cards used in the trick are picked up and placed to one side. Since, as will be explained in the following examples, a trick will always use all the cards on the table the next player must play a card to an empty table.

Examples:

1. The table contains a 2 and a 0. The player uses another 0 from his hand and arranges the cards thus:

$$200$$

scoring 200 by simple arrangement.

2. The table contains a 9 and an 8. The player uses a 2 from his hand and can arrange the cards in either of the following ways:

98	or	92
2		8
(100)		(100)

which, by addition, scores 100.

    If, in this case, there is also a 5 and a 3 on the table, they can be added to the left of the number as shown:

5398	or	5392
2		8
(5400)		(5400)

increasing the score to 5400.

3. The table contains a 1 and a 0. The player uses a 9 from his hand and arranges the cards in either of the following ways:

10	or	90
9		1
(100)		(100)

scoring 100.

    In this case the lower card is placed in the tens position, the following 0 being understood. This can be done with more than one row providing, however, there is always a real 0.

For example:

$$
\begin{array}{c}
60 \\
3 \\
\underline{21} \\
(300)
\end{array}
$$

4. The table contains a 1, 2, 2, 3, and 4. The player uses a 7 from his hand and arranges the cards as follows (which is one of many possible arrangements, all of which add up to 100):

$$
\begin{array}{c}
31 \\
27 \\
\underline{42} \\
(100)
\end{array}
$$

5. Examples 2 and 4 show the most usual way of forming tricks, by having the units column add up to 10 while the tens column adds up to 9. Another way is to have the units column add up to 20 while the tens column adds up to 8. For example:

$$\begin{array}{r} 76 \\ 15 \\ \underline{9} \\ (100) \end{array}$$

It is possible, although very rare, to have the units column add up to 30 while the tens column adds up to 7.

● *Winning the game.* The first team to reach 10,000 or more points is the winner. As soon as it is reached the game is over.

If all the cards are played from the hands before 10,000 is reached, a new hand is dealt by the next dealer, the cards remaining on the table being picked up without scoring.

● *The game for two.* Deal six cards to each player. As each player plays a card he replaces it from the deck. When the deck is exhausted the remaining six cards are played out.

All rules of play are the same as in the game for four.

I'LL END THIS CHAPTER on hunting with the biggest game of them all, found in the reference library of the Essex Institute in Salem, Massachusetts. It is ALDIBORONTIPHOSKYPHORNIOSTIKOS, from a little book of the same name by R. Stennett published in 1825. The game isn't much, simply the paying of forfeits for mispronouncing words in passages read from the book, but the name is certainly imposing, surpassing MUSINAYKAHWHANMETOWAYWIN, the Cree and Chippewa version of FOX AND GEESE.

Two
GAME INVENTORS
Are
PEOPLE
Too

Early in the seventeenth century Sir John Suckling, an English poet, invented a game that has been played by countless millions ever since. In 1909, Elwood T. Baker, a Brooklyn WHIST teacher, created another that is now undoubtedly the most popular two-hand card game around. The first game is CRIBBAGE and the second is GIN RUMMY, but how many of the fans of either of these games could identify the inventor?

Even when the creator of a game is a matter of historical record, and this is rarely the case, the vast majority of the players of that game couldn't care less. They (with the exception of many CHESS addicts) are just not interested in the origins of their game. This indifference is reflected in the attitude of scholars who, when writing about a civilization, will scrutinize every aspect in minute detail but will dismiss the games played by that civilization as trivial or, going to the other extreme, as too intricate to be comprehended.

In my opinion, which is definitely not unbiased, a game is a work of art as worthy of being signed as a painting, a book, or a musical composition. This is not practical in the case of games that have evolved through numerous changes. And it is impossible where the creator's name has been irretrievably lost. But certainly in the case of games being created today—and this is the most productive time in the history of games—the inventor should have the right, and the obligation, to sign his work.

This chapter will consist of games contributed by ten of my very creative friends. Most of these friends are professionals, not in the sense that they earn their living from games (only one does) but because they have taken the time and the effort to learn their craft and then have practiced it, turning out a steady flow of finished work.

I am the president and chief archivist of a very informal group with a very formal name: "New York Game Associates," or N.Y.G.A., for short. At irregular intervals we meet and present new games for approval, and for criticism.

Three of the games in this chapter, and many of my own games in the following chapters, spring directly from the stimulating N.Y.G.A. atmosphere.

Claude Soucie, a charter member of N.Y.G.A., is the father of seven charming children and the creator of such delightful family games as SPLIT PERSONALITY, KNIFE YOUR BUDDY, and BIG FUNERAL. Claude is also a humorist and has, as the above titles indicate, often successfully blended both facets of his personality in his work.

Claude's game of WATCH, published by the Campaign Game Company, is not in a humorous vein but, for a game of pure skill, has a light touch that allows just about any age level to enjoy it. Another plus: a game takes about five minutes to play.

LINES OF ACTION (LOA) is also a game of pure skill. It can be played on a checkerboard, but it presents a new manner of moving the pieces and, something much harder to find, a novel objective. Claude also has a version that can be played by from two to six players on a special board. This, hopefully, will be available to the public in the near future.

LINES OF ACTION (LOA)　　　*by Claude Soucie*

● *Number of players.* Two.

● *Equipment.* A checkerboard and twelve pieces for each player. The pieces are set up, as shown, on the outer spaces of the board, one player having the black pieces and the other having the white.

● *The play.* Black moves first. Play then alternates. A piece moves in a straight line, including diagonally, *exactly* as many spaces as there are pieces, enemy or friendly, including the piece moved, in that straight line. (For example, Black, at the beginning of the game, could move his piece A to space B, C, or D.)

A piece can move over one or more friendly pieces, but cannot land on a space occupied by a friendly piece. The pieces passed over are not affected in any way. (For example, let us say that Black's first move is piece A to space D and that White then moves piece E to space F. Black could now move piece G three spaces to space H, passing over his own piece. Black could also move piece G five spaces to the left to space I, passing over three of his own pieces. There are other moves, of course, that piece G could make. Piece J could not move five spaces to the left since this would cause it to land on a black piece.)

A piece cannot move over an enemy piece. It may, however, land on the same space as the enemy piece, thereby capturing it and removing it from the game. (Following the previous example, if Black has moved a piece to space D, White could not move piece K three spaces to the left, passing over the black piece. White could, however, move piece L two spaces diagonally to capture the piece on position D.)

● *Winning the game.* A player has a winning position when all of his remaining pieces have been gathered into one connected group. The connection between pieces in the group can be either orthogonal or diagonal.

If a player is reduced, by captures, to one remaining piece, that piece constitutes a winning position.

When a player, by making a capture, creates a winning position for himself and at the same time, by eliminating an isolated piece, creates a winning position for his opponent, the victory goes to the player making the move.

● *A sample end game.* The following ending of an actual game shows some of the richness of position that can develop in LOA.

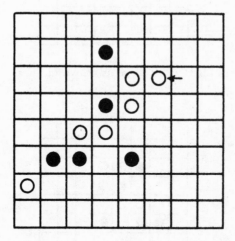

In the position shown, if it were Black's turn to play he could win the game by moving his topmost piece down three spaces, capturing a white piece, and uniting all of his, Black's, pieces.

However it is White's turn and he moves the piece indicated by the arrow to the position shown in the following diagram.

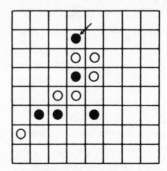

Black, blocked from an immediate win, moves the indicated piece to the position shown below.

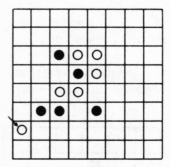

White moves his isolated piece as shown in the next diagram.

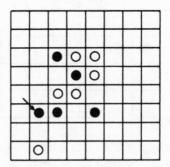

White threatens to win by moving two spaces directly upward. Black parries the threat by moving his piece to the position shown in the following diagram.

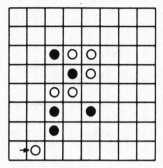

White's upward move is now reduced to one space. Instead he moves the piece horizontally. (He is not permitted to jump over the black piece.)

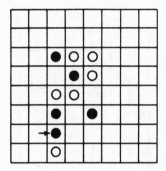

White again threatens a win by moving two spaces diagonally upward and Black interposes by moving the piece indicated.

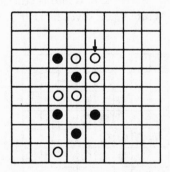

Black can now win by moving his topmost piece two spaces down diagonally and White counters by capturing a black piece, jumping over his own piece.

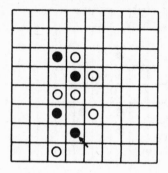

Black, in no immediate danger, moves the piece shown up to the left.

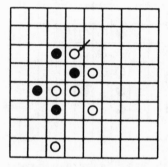

Black again threatens to win by moving his second piece from the top two spaces to the left. And White is still not able to connect up his isolated piece. White again saves himself by capturing a black piece.

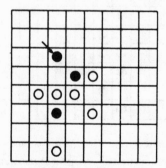

Black continues his attack by moving the indicated piece.

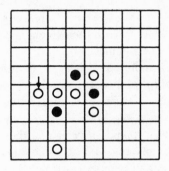

Black is once more in position to win by moving his bottom piece to the right. White stops this by adding another piece to the line, changing the move of the black piece to three.

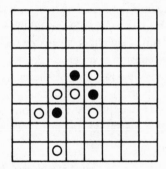

Black is blocked from moving to the right. He also cannot stop White from moving one space diagonally up to the left, winning the game.

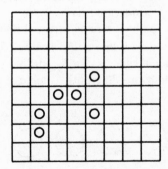

White's winning position (with the black pieces not shown).

Among the founders of N.Y.G.A. are Arthur and Wald Amberstone, a father and son team. They earn their living making baskets, an odd job, they say, like making games.

Power, one of their more epic games, is an attempt to model their own playful philosophy of history. Another of their creations, the "High Deck," is a beautiful new set of cards based on the hierarchical relationships of society in the Middle Ages.

Their game of Cups is a modern version of the oldest known game, Mancala. Boards for playing Mancala have been found carved in the stonework of Egyptian temples constructed more than 3000 years ago. Despite its antiquity it is still very much alive. It is without question the national game of Africa and has been spread, as a part of the Moslem culture, as far east as the Philippines.

The equipment for playing Mancala varies with the people playing it. Often the board is simply a series of cups hollowed in the ground. More advanced boards are carved in wood and in some tribes are true works of art. Among forest dwellers, beans or seeds usually serve as playing pieces, while coastal dwellers make use of small shells or pebbles. Desert nomads, lacking any of these, have been known to make do with pellets of dried camel dung.

Cups at first glance is deceptively simple but with repeated play the many subtleties of the strategy begin to emerge.

CUPS   *by Arthur and Wald Amberstone*

* *Number of players.* Two.
* *Equipment.* Ten containers. (Many household objects can be pressed into service, tops from discarded jars being particularly convenient. If possible, eight should be of roughly the same size, while two should be considerably larger.)

Eighty beans, preferably equally divided between two colors. (While the term "bean" will be used in the description of the game, any fairly uniform small objects can be utilized. For my own set I purchased and unstrung two differently colored strings of inexpensive plastic beads.)

● *The setup.* The ten containers are arranged in two lines to form a board as shown. The smaller containers are known as cups, while the larger ones are called pots.

The players are seated across from each other and each plays only in the line nearer to him.

Each player receives forty beans, which he either keeps in hand or stores in some convenient place other than the board. These are his stock. Choose for first play in any convenient manner.

● *The play.* Each player in turn has a choice of doing one of the following:

1. Remove 1, 2, 3, or 4 beans from his stock and place them in his line of cups. The first bean is always placed in the cup at the left end of his line (farthest from his pot) and, if more than one is played, the others are placed in adjacent cups, one bean in each, to the right (toward the pot).

2. Take the contents from one cup and "sow" (this being a term used in MANCALA) all of the beans, one at a time, in adjacent cups to the right until the last bean is placed in the pot. In order to be able to do this the cup must contain just the right number of beans, such as 1 bean in the cup next to the pot up to 4 beans in the farthest cup.

● *Blocked cups.* When a cup has more beans in it than the number required to reach the pot by sowing, it is blocked and cannot be emptied by the player. (This puts the player in a vulnerable position and, except for unusual strategic considerations, should be avoided. In other words be sure that your "cup runneth not over.")

● *Capturing beans.* When a player places beans from his stock so that the last bean lands in an empty cup, the contents, if any, of the opposite cup in his opponent's line are captured and placed in the player's pot.

● *Ending the game.* After a player has placed all the beans from his stock he continues, in turn, by making sowing plays, if possible. When a player has no further plays, his opponent can continue to make whatever plays are still available to him.

When all plays have been made the game is over. Beans left in the cups belong to neither player. The player with the most beans in his pot is the winner and if both players have the same number, it is a tie.

• A *sample game*. The following start of a game was set up to illustrate the various types of plays, and by no means represents the most skillful tactics.

B stands for the bottom player in the diagram and T the top. The arrows show their direction of placing and sowing beans.

B places 1 bean.

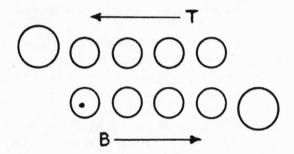

T places 4 beans. The fourth is placed in an empty cup. The 1 bean in the opposite cup is captured and placed in T's pot.

B places 3 beans, also making a capture.

T places 2 beans, making a second capture.

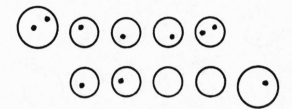

B places 1 bean.

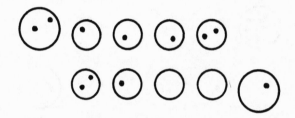

T empties the cup next to his pot and sows the bean in his pot.

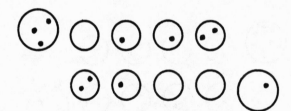

B places 2 beans.

T places 4 beans, making a capture of 3 beans from the opposite cup.

B also places 4 beans and captures 3 beans.

T removes the 2 beans from the cup two away from his pot and sows them. He has now blocked the cup next to his pot.

B sows the contents of the cup adjacent to his pot.

T places 3 beans, making another capture of 3 beans.

B places 1 bean.

T empties his cup with 3 beans and sows them.

At this point *T* is ahead with 11 beans in his pot compared to 5 in *B*'s. However because of *T*'s blocked cup, *B* has potentially the better game.

● *Different numbers of cups.* The game so far described, with each player having four cups, is the ideal size for initially becoming acquainted with the beauties of Cups. After this has been accomplished, players can experiment with greater numbers of cups, up to ten on a side. Or they can move in the opposite direction, the game with three cups on a side making a delightful miniature.

Whatever the number of cups used, each player receives 10 beans per cup as his stock. Thus when playing with ten cups on a side, each player starts with 100 beans; and with three cups on a side the initial stock is 30 beans.

BOB ABBOTT IS THE AUTHOR, logically enough, of *Abbott's New Card Games*. This book consists of eight original card games and a stowaway, ULTIMA, which is a board game that makes CHESS seem like child's play.

ELEUSIS, one of the best of the games, is unique in being the only card game, except for several derived from it, which is based on inductive rather than deductive reasoning. This means that, unlike the usual game where the rules are known and the player strives in his play to use them to best advantage, in ELEUSIS the player's objective is to discover the rules.

ELEUSIS created a considerable stir in the scientific world when first featured in the "Mathematical Games" department of the June 1959 *Scientific American*. And this interest is still very much alive.

Bob's other published game goes to the opposite extreme and is based on pure deductive logic. WHAT'S THAT ON MY HEAD?, published by Games Research, is a takeoff on the classic problem of the sultan who tests the wits of his wisest men by painting colored circles on their foreheads.

In the last few years Bob has been confining his creativity to a very successful career as a computer programmer and has, only temporarily we hope, abandoned games. As a parting gift to N.Y.G.A. he came up with CROSSINGS. This is a fast-paced checkerboard battle featuring a novel type of move that can best be described as a surge forward.

CROSSINGS   *by Robert Abbott*

● *Number of players*. Two.

● *Equipment*. A checkerboard. Sixteen white and 16 black pieces. The pieces are set up in the two rows nearest to the players, using spaces of both colors. (See diagram 1 of sample game.)

Diagram 1

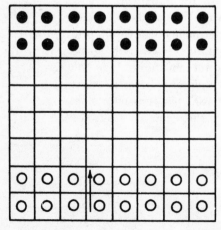

Diagram 2

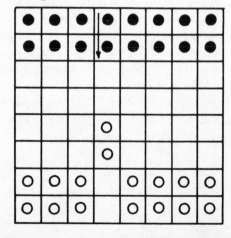

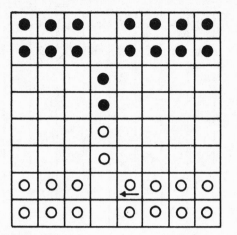

Diagram 3

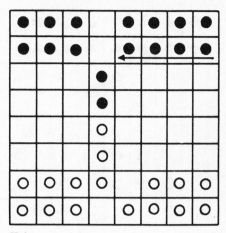

Diagram 4

• *The play.* White makes the first move. Play then alternates.

A single piece can move one space in any direction, including diagonally, to an unoccupied square. (See diagrams 18–19 and 19–20.)

Two or more pieces adjacent to each other in a straight line, including diagonally, can all move together in the direction of the straight line, one or more spaces, up to a maximum of the number of pieces in the moving group. (See diagrams 1–2 for an example of 2 pieces moving together a maximum of two spaces. See diagrams 4–5 for an example of 4 pieces moving one space together.)

It is not necessary for an entire group of adjacent pieces to be moved. Instead one or more pieces at the end of the group may be moved separately, the maximum number of spaces being determined by the number of pieces actually moved. (See diagrams 3–4 and 7–8.)

Diagram 5

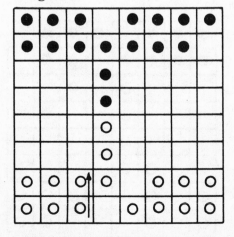

Diagram 6

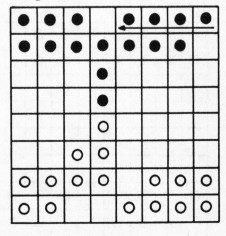

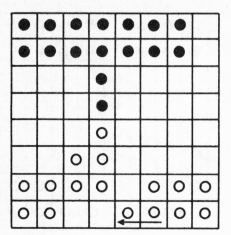

Diagram 7

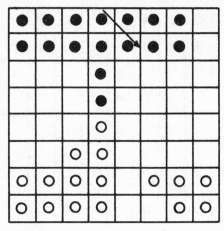

Diagram 8

• *Capturing.* When a moving group of pieces runs into a single enemy piece or an enemy group in the same line, that is smaller, the first encountered enemy piece can be captured. Only one piece can be captured even though the group would otherwise have been able to move farther. A capture cannot be made if the enemy group is equal to or larger than the moving group.

(In diagram 8 the two groups of 4 pieces facing each other are equal, so neither may capture the other. In diagram 9, however, Black has reduced his group to 3 and White now captures a piece, as shown completed in diagram 10. Diagrams 12–13 show a capture of a single piece by a group of 2. Diagrams 14–15 show a capture after moving through two vacant spaces.)

• *Crossings.* When a player succeeds in moving a piece across the board to the farthest row, he has made a "crossing." Unless the op-

Diagram 9

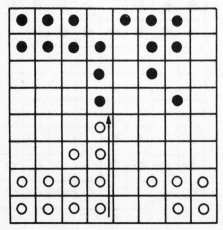

Diagram 10

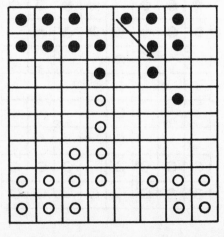

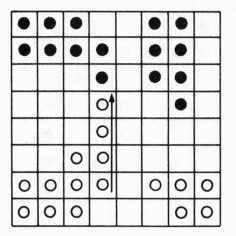

Diagram 11

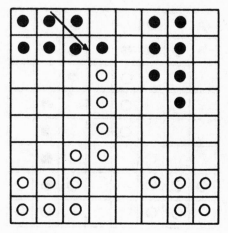

Diagram 12

ponent can respond immediately with another crossing, the game is over, won by the original player.

If a crossing is countered by an enemy crossing, they cancel each other and the game continues. The crossed pieces must remain where they are and can be neither moved by their owner nor captured by the opponent.

(Black in diagram 17 completes a crossing which is countered by White in diagram 18. A similar pair occur in diagrams 19–20 and also in diagrams 23–24.)

* *A sample game.* Since the method of moving and capturing in CROSSINGS is so unusual, I have decided to illustrate it with a complete game as played between Bob Abbott and myself. (None of your business who played Black.)

The arrow in each diagram shows the piece or pieces that are being moved and the succeeding diagram shows the position after the move.

Diagram 13

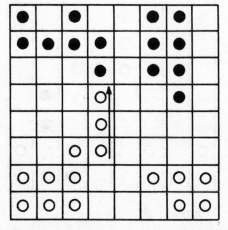

Diagram 14

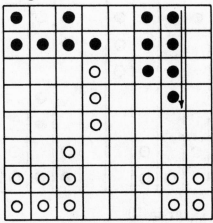

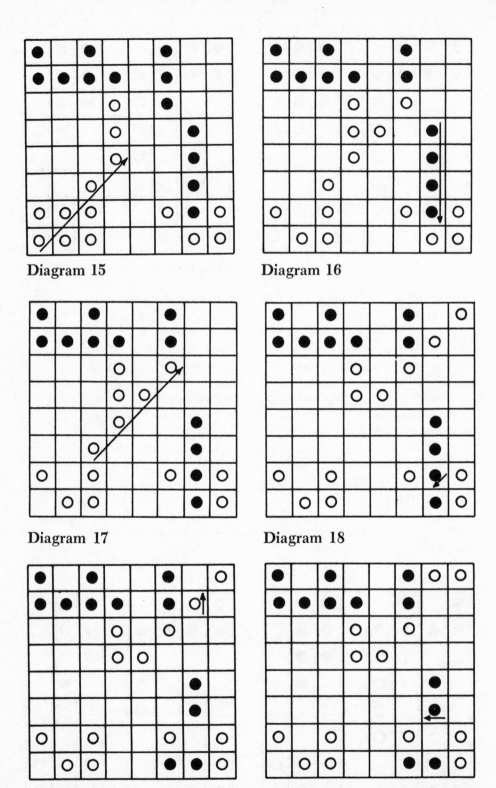

Diagram 15

Diagram 16

Diagram 17

Diagram 18

Diagram 19

Diagram 20

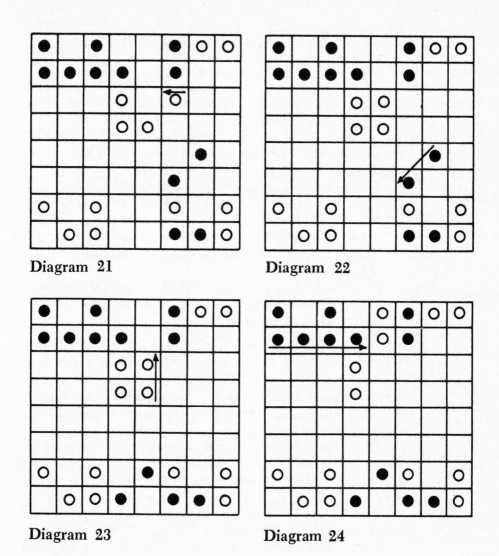

Diagram 21

Diagram 22

Diagram 23

Diagram 24

At this point White resigns. Black will capture his piece as shown by the arrow. White can then stop an immediate Black crossing by moving his single piece back to block the way. But, barring a serious misplay by Black, White has no chance of winning.

ABOUT A YEAR AGO I received a letter from Poland which began as follows:

> It could be a shock, really, getting a letter like this one, from a faraway country and an unknown person. This mystery needs to be explained at once.
>
> Your name and address I have got from Robert Abbott, who wrote me: "Sid has several games on the market, he knows more about the history of games than anyone in this country and he is presently working on a couple of books about games . . ."
>
> I have not had the pleasure of meeting Mr. Abbott personally; I wrote him a letter after reading his book about new card games invented by him. The reason for this nervous activity of mine is simple: I wrote a book on games myself. It is a history of board games (including modern ones and excluding Chess). Now I am writing a companion volume on playing cards, and steadily gathering new information on board games for the second improved edition of my book . . .

This, thanks to Bob Abbott, was my introduction to Lech Pijanowski of Warsaw, Poland. Lech is a film critic by profession and, ever since being bitten by the same bug that got me, an avid game nut. Our correspondence has been lengthy, fruitful, and a source of great satisfaction to me. In another twenty years we might begin to exhaust the information we have to impart to each other.

Lech, in addition to his books, writes a weekly newspaper column on the various aspects of games. From one of the very attractive clippings he sent to me I translated (with considerable difficulty, Polish being a rough language for a beginner) the following game of LAP. The name has no significance since he took the inventor's prerogative of simply forming it from his initials.

LAP is a second or third cousin to the well-known pencil and paper game of BATTLESHIPS. It, however, offers much more scope for strategic planning in gathering information and for deductive reasoning in interpreting the information once gathered.

And so, with Lech's kind permission . . .

● *Number of players.* Two.

● *Equipment.* A pencil and sheet of graph paper for each player.

● *The setup.* On his sheet of paper each player outlines two 8 × 8 squares, containing sixty-four cells. The cells in the squares are identified by numbering from 1 to 8 along the top of a square and from A to H along the side of a square.

The players, keeping their papers out of sight of each other, divide one of their squares into four continuous sectors which are labeled I, II, III, and IV. The sectors must each contain sixteen cells but may be as irregular in shape as the player wishes. The second square is used for reconstructing the opponent's sectors as information about them is obtained.

The next two diagrams are examples of dividing a square.

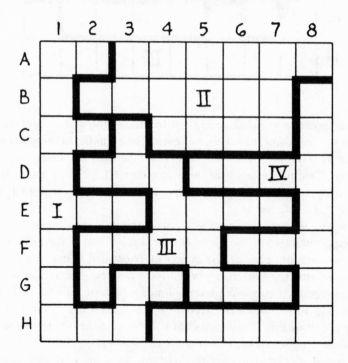

● *Getting information.* Each player in turn calls out the coordinates of four cells which are located together in the form of a 2 × 2 square. This is done by mentioning two letters and two numbers. A call of C-D-2-3 would represent cells C2, C3, D2, and D3.

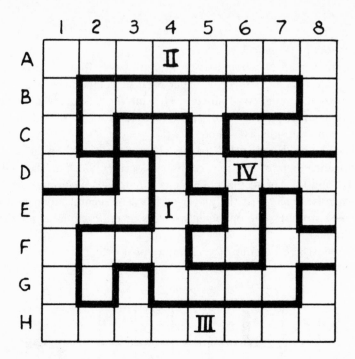

The opponent responds to the call by stating the sectors contained in the four cells and the number of each. For example, to the previous call of C-D-2-3 the owner of the first of the sample squares would answer, "One in sector I and three in sector III." The owner of the second square would respond to the same call with, "One each in sectors I, II, III, and IV."

• *Winning the game.* As soon as a player thinks he has reconstructed his opponent's sectors the game is over, except that if the opponent was the second to play he, the opponent, is entitled to one more call.

A reconstructed pattern to be correct must be exactly the same as the original. If only one player submits a pattern, he wins or loses depending on whether it is correct or not. If both submit patterns the game is a draw if both are correct or if both are incorrect. If only one has a correct pattern he, of course, is the winner.

• *A few words on deducing the pattern.* To show how one might tackle the problem let's work on the second sample given above. If we call A-B-1-2 we will learn that these four cells consist of three in sector II and one in sector IV. A call of A-B-2-3 nets the information that two are in sector II and two are in sector IV. And B-C-1-2 gives the same result. Putting these facts together the following are some of the possible ways the eight cells we have asked about can be arranged:

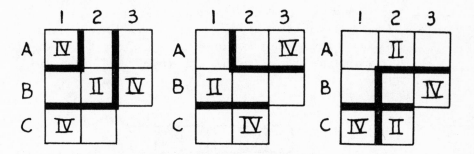

The first diagram obviously can't meet the criterion that all sectors must be continuous.

The second looks as if it might work, but a little study will show that in order for sector IV to join up it would take more than sixteen cells to enclose sixteen cells of sector II.

Number three is out because it is not possible for both sectors to be made continuous.

So eliminating these possibilities and their mirror images we are left with the only correct pattern, as follows:

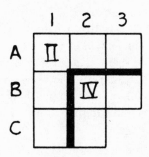

We are now sure of these eight cells, but we have taken three calls to pin them down. As you gain experience in playing LAP you will learn how to spread your calls over wide areas and then mesh all the data into one glorious revelation. And that, of course, is the beauty of the game.

It was also through Bob Abbott that I became acquainted with Haar Hoolim, a prolific Israeli inventor of games. Haar, originally from Canada, is now in retirement at Migdal Ascalon where he spends much of his time "studying" games. His "studies" take the form of a steady flow of new game ideas since, unlike Lech Pijanowski and myself, Haar is primarily interested in his own creations.

One of Haar's most important creations is a set of CHINESE MATCHING CARDS. There are thirty-six cards in the set similar to the following four, each containing a different arrangement of light and dark squares.

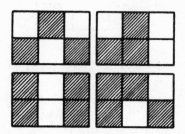

Haar has devised dozens of unique games to be played with the CHINESE MATCHING CARDS and fifteen of them have been published, together with a set of the cards, by the Adult Leisure Products Corporation. This is sold, quite appropriately, under the name HAAR HOOLIM PERCEPTION GAMES.

During the five years that I have been corresponding with Haar I have received a mountain of written material from him. Buried in this mountain are many game gems waiting to be excavated and polished. THREE MUSKETEERS, however, was found sparkling at the surface and certainly needed no polishing. It is a short game, taking ten minutes at the most to play. But it is a game that you will want to play again and again.

THREE MUSKETEERS   *by Haar Hoolim*

● *Number of players.* Two.
● *Equipment.* A 5 × 5 board as shown on the next page. This can simply be sketched on a piece of paper to be discarded at the end of the session or a more permanent board can be drawn on cardboard.

Three pieces of one color, known as the Three Musketeers, and 22 pieces of a contrasting color, known as the Enemy. Two sets of checkers can be used, or poker chips, or even coins. To start the game the pieces are placed on the board as shown.

• *The play.* The player with the Three Musketeers always moves first and play then alternates. Each player in turn moves one piece.

A Musketeer can be moved to any adjacent (not including diagonally) space which is occupied by an Enemy piece, the Enemy piece being removed from the game. (Thus at the start, each corner Musketeer has two spaces it can move to, while the center Musketeer has four possibilities.)

An Enemy piece can be moved to any adjacent (not including diagonally) vacant space.

• *Object of play.* The Enemy attempts to force the Three Musketeers onto the same row or column (where it is assumed they can be captured) and wins as soon as the Musketeers are so positioned.

The Musketeers win if on their turn to move there is no move available because there is no Enemy piece adjacent to a Musketeer and, of course, they have not as yet been forced onto a single row or column.

• *Scoring variation.* In playing a series of games it adds interest to use one of the following two scoring systems. An even number of games should be played so that each player has the same number of chances at each side.

1. If the contestant playing the Enemy pieces wins, he scores 1 point for each Enemy piece remaining on the board. If the contestant playing the Musketeers wins, he scores 10 points.

2. If the contestant playing the Enemy pieces wins, he scores 10 points minus 1 for each Enemy piece remaining on the board. Thus if there are more than 10 Enemy pieces remaining on the board, the player will end up losing points. If the contestant playing the Musketeers wins, he scores 10 points.

To keep the Musketeers from deliberately ending the game to their advantage the rule is added that the Three Musketeers may not be moved onto a single row or column if any other move is available to them.

● *A sample end game.* For recording a game the spaces are numbered as shown in the following diagram. A designation such as 32–42 indicates that the piece in space 32 moves to space 42. When a Musketeer moves, it automatically makes a capture.

White (the Enemy) has 8 pieces left and it is his turn to move. If the game were being played by the scoring rules of variation (1), the play could be as follows. (It will be easier to follow the example if the pieces are set up on a board and moved as indicated.)

Move	Black	White
1	———	32–42
2	52–42	33–43
3	42–43	34–35
4	45–35	24–34
5	35–34	14–24
6	34–24	13–23
7	24–23	

The Musketeers are now on one column, as shown below, and White scores 2 points, since two Enemy pieces remain on the board.

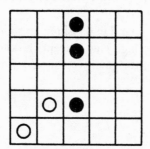

If the game were being played by the scoring rules of variation (2), the play could be as follows.

Move	Black	White
1	———	34–35
2	45–35	24–25
3	35–25	14–15
4	25–15	13–14
5	15–14	32–42
6	52–42	22–32
7	42–32	11–12
8	32–33	12–13
9	14–13	

The final position is as shown below and White has won a maximum score of 10 points, since there are no Enemy pieces remaining.

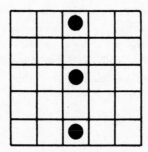

Phil Laurence is a structural engineer who, as I see it, devotes much too much time to engineering and not nearly enough time to creating games. To be sure he is an expert on nuclear power plants and his know-how is an important plus in protecting us against the dangers of explosion and radiation. But I would love to see him come up with more games like Paks.

As an old pro I had a hand in polishing up some of the rough edges, particularly in the scoring. The concept, however, is entirely Phil's and it has a delightful originality that makes it different from any other card game.

PAKS   *by Phil Laurence*

● *Number of players.* Paks is equally exciting for two, three, four, or six players. With two or three players it's every man for himself. With four or six players, divide into two teams, partners being seated alternately.

● *The deck.* For a two-hand game use a standard deck of fifty-two cards. When more than two play, form a 104-card deck by shuffling together two standard decks. If the backs don't match, it won't interfere with the game.

● *The deal.* Cut for first deal, high card receiving the honor. In subsequent hands the deal rotates to the left.

The dealer presents the deck to the player on his right for cutting and then passes out five cards to each player, including himself, one at a time. Three cards are placed face up in the center of the table and the undealt portion of the deck is then placed face down next to the three "table cards," completing the deal.

● *The draw.* The player to the left of the dealer plays first. He draws the top card from the stock (undealt portion of the deck) and shows it. If it is of a different suit from any of the table cards he must add it to the table cards and his turn ends. If the drawn card matches a table card in suit he places the drawn card in his hand and can then either end his play or continue as described under *Making Paks.*

Play rotates to the left.

(As an example of the draw, let us suppose the table cards to be the ♠6, ♡10, and ♣Q. If a player draws the ♢5, he must place it on the table—this is known as "feeding the table." If he draws the ♡8, however, he adds it to his hand.)

• *Value of the cards.* PAKS is a game of using cards from the hand to take others from the table, and in this connection each card has a counting value as follows:

Ace ——————————————20 points
King, Queen, or Jack —————10 points
10 through 2 ——the number of the card

Certain "combinations" of cards of the same suit take on an increased value. These combinations and their values are as follows:

5 and 5 ——————————————55 points
5 and 4 ——————————————54 points
5 and 3 ——————————————53 points
5 and 2 ——————————————52 points
4 and 4 ——————————————44 points
4 and 3 ——————————————43 points
4 and 2 ——————————————42 points
3 and 3 ——————————————33 points
3 and 2 ——————————————32 points
2 and 2 ——————————————22 points

(Combinations of 5 and 5, 4 and 4, 3 and 3, and 2 and 2 are not possible when using only one deck.)

Combinations have their added value only when held and played from the hand. Once on the table they return to their basic counting value.

• *Making Paks.* When a player adds a card to his hand (see *The draw*), he may continue by making a Pak. This is done by using one or more cards of the same suit from his hand to take a table card, also of the same suit. The cards played from the hand must have a value greater than that of the card taken. The difference may be as little as 1 point or as great as the player wishes.

The group of cards so formed is called a Pak and is placed face up near the player and spread so that the value is clearly evident.

It is not necessary to use the originally drawn card as one of the cards of the Pak.

Only one Pak can be made on a turn.

If in subsequent turns a player makes additional Paks of the same suit, each is kept separate.

(As an example of making Paks, let us suppose the table cards to be ♠A, ♠5, ♡Q, and ♢8. A player draws the ♡6, shows it to the other players, and adds it to his hand. He then decides to make a Pak and chooses spades as the suit.

His hand contains the following spades: King, 10, 6, 3, 2. He can take either the ♠A or ♠5, but is not allowed to take both. The 6 is sufficient to take the 5, but more cards can be added if the player desires. To take the Ace he needs the King, 10, and one other card since an Ace counts 20 and King plus 10 also counts 20. He can also use the 3, 2 combination, with a value of 32 points when played from the hand, to take either card.

If he uses the 3, 2 combination to take the Ace, the value of the Pak becomes 25, since the 3 and 2 revert to their basic counting value.)

• *Full table.* When, at a player's turn, the table contains at least one card of each of the four suits, it is known as a "full table." The player draws as usual but adds the card to his hand without showing it. He *must* now make a Pak.

If the cards in his hand are such that he cannot possibly make a Pak in any suit, he shows his hand to the other players for verification and that ends his turn. The next player is consequently faced with a full table.

• *Stealing Paks.* After a player has drawn and made a Pak, he may, if he wishes, continue by stealing one or more Paks from other players. Stealing a Pak is accomplished in the same manner as making a Pak, by playing from the hand a card or cards of the same suit and greater in value than the stolen Pak.

If a single opponent has more than one Pak of the same suit, as many may be stolen at one time as the value of the cards from the hand permits. (For example: an opponent has three Paks in diamonds, one worth 14, one worth 25, and one worth 43. ♢J, ♢3, and ♢2—for a total value of 42 points—could take the first two. While ♢5, ♢4, ♢3, and ♢2, which can be played as 53 and 42, could take all three.) The stolen Paks are combined, together with the cards from the hand, to make one new Pak. However, if the player doing the stealing already has a Pak or Paks of the same suit, they are kept separate.

In any one turn, a player is limited to only one play in each suit. Thus, if he starts by making a Pak in hearts, he cannot steal in hearts, but may steal up to three Paks, one in each of the other three suits. He may steal from different opponents or all from one opponent.

In a partnership game it is permissible (though rarely strategically desirable) to steal a Pak from a partner.

● *Note.* A player must first draw and keep a card in order to be able to play. (Feeding the table ends his turn.)

He may then make a Pak.

With a full table he must make a Pak.

Only after drawing and keeping a card, and then making a Pak, may a player continue by stealing a Pak or Paks.

● *When the deck is exhausted.* Since every play must start with the drawing of a card, no further plays can be made after the deck is exhausted. Any cards remaining in a player's hand are discarded, but do not count against him.

● *Throwing off Paks.* After play is finished, each player (or team, for a four- or six-hand game) counts the number of Paks he has in each suit. Taking each suit separately each player (or team) must throw off a number of Paks equal to that held by the player (or team) with the least amount.

(For example, in a four-hand game, team A has five Paks in spades while team B has two Paks in spades. Each team must throw off two spade Paks, regardless of their value; though team A will naturally choose the two with the lowest values. The remaining 3 spade Paks are counted for team A, team B receiving no score in spades.)

(As another example, in a three-hand game, player A has three diamond Paks, player B has four diamond Paks, and player C has one diamond Pak. Each must throw off one diamond Pak. If player C had no diamond Paks, players A and B would not have to throw off any.)

● *Scoring.* After throwing off, each player or team counts and scores the value of all their remaining cards. To simplify the counting round out the value of the cards as follows:

Ace ——————————— 20 points
K, Q, J, 10, 9, 8 ———— 10 points
7, 6, 5, 4, 3, 2 ————— 5 points

The first player or team to reach 500 points wins the game. In case of a tie at or above 500 points, play another hand to break the tie.

THE MAIN DELIGHT of any hobby is sharing it with others of a similar interest. While it is true that there are a lot less people who make a hobby of games than, say, stamps, I have found those who do choose games to be a most fascinating group.

One such game enthusiast is Father Daniel, of the Benedictine Order, who resides in an abbey in Benet Lake, Wisconsin. I haven't as yet had the pleasure of meeting him in person but we have shared a lengthy and stimulating correspondence.

Father Daniel is a game inventor with a penchant for figures, the mathematical kind. Although his game of NUMBER FOOTBALL uses only pencils and a special pad, it is most successful in capturing the skill and thrill of the parent game. A rule booklet together with the special pad can be purchased directly from the abbey.

SKEDOODLE is another of Father Daniel's number games. It is ideal for "skedoodling" around with a pencil and a piece of paper, and a few minutes to kill. The basic idea is simple, intriguing, and lends itself to an endless series of variations. And deriving new variations can be half the fun of the game.

SKEDOODLE   *by Father Daniel*

● *Number of players.* Two, three, or four.
● *Equipment.* A pencil for each player and one sheet of paper.
● *Preliminary.* Before each game the players together agree on one of the following numbers to be the "master number" for that game: 3, 4, 5, 6, 7, 8, or 9. Any number containing the chosen number, or any two-digit number which by adding, subtracting, multiplying, or dividing the two digits results in the chosen number, will score for the player writing it (as explained in *The play*).

All of this may sound a little complicated but an example should clear it up. Let us say that 4 is chosen as the "master number." Writing a 4, 14, or 24 would score because each contains the number 4. 13 would score by addition $(1 + 3 = 4)$; 15 by subtraction $(5 - 1 = 4)$; 22 by addition or multiplication $(2 + 2 = 4$ or $2 \times 2 = 4)$; 26 by subtraction $(6 - 2 = 4)$; and 28 by division $(8 \div 2 = 4)$.
● *The play.* Choose the first player in any convenient manner. The one so chosen begins by writing any number from 1 to 30, except a scoring number.

The next player then writes a number which he derives from the first number and play continues with each player in turn deriving a number from the number written by the preceding player. All numbers must be whole numbers between 1 and 30 and may not duplicate a previously used number.

Numbers are derived by one of the following operations:

1. Adding, subtracting, multiplying, or dividing the digits of a two-digit number. (For example, 28 could be used to derive 10 by addition, 6 by subtraction, 16 by multiplication, or 4 by division.)
2. Doubling (as 9 to 18)
3. Halving (as 22 to 11)
4. Squaring (as 4 to 16)
5. Taking the square root (as 16 to 4)
6. From the number 1 any unused number can be derived.

● *Ending the game.* When a player cannot legally derive a number which has not been used before, the game is ended. Each player scores 1 point for each scoring number he has written and the player with the highest total is the winner.

● *A sample game.* Two players are competing and choose 4 as the "master number."

A starts by writing ——————————————17
By subtraction (7 − 1), B derives ———————— 6
By halving, A derives ——————————————— 3
By squaring, B derives ——————————————— 9
By doubling, A derives ——————————————18
By subtraction, B derives —————————————— 7
By doubling, A derives ——————————————14 and scores
By multiplication (1 × 4), B derives ———— 4 and scores
By squaring, A derives ——————————————16
By subtraction, B derives —————————————— 5
By squaring, A derives ——————————————25
By multiplication, B derives ————————————10
By doubling, A derives ——————————————20
By addition (2 + 0), B derives ———————— 2
By halving, A derives ——————————————— 1
From 1, B chooses to go to ———————————15 and scores
By doubling, A derives ——————————————30

No unused number can now be derived and B wins the game by a score of 2 to 1.

● *Variations.* The following are a few variations I have devised on the basic theme. Try them, and then have fun coming up with your own.

1. In a two-player game, one player secretly chooses a "master number" while the other secretly chooses a starting number. If the sum of these two numbers is even, the player who chose the "master number" plays first. If the sum is odd, the player who chose the starting number plays first. Whoever plays first of course starts with the chosen number.

2. As well as 1, 10 and any two-digit number that adds up to 10 (such as 19 and 28) can be used to derive any unused number the player chooses.

3. Instead of choosing a "master number," choose two or more numbers and score only when these numbers actually appear in the written number. (For example, if 2 and 5 are chosen the following numbers would each score 1 point: 2, 5, 12, 15, 20, 21, 23, 24, 26, 27, 28, and 29. 22 and 25 would each score 2 points.

4. To the other legal methods of deriving a number, add a shift number. This number, chosen before the play begins, can be added to or subtracted from the given number to derive a new number. (For example, if 3 is chosen as the shift number, 16 could be shifted to either 19 or 13.)

5. The player who writes the final number of a game is penalized 1 point. When playing a high scoring variation, this penalty can be raised to 2 or even 3 points.

6. For a longer game more numbers can be used, such as 40, 50, etc., up to a maximum of 99.

● *Combining variations.* All kinds of combinations can be made of the above variations, as for example the following game which is a combination of (3) and (4).

Again two players are competing. They choose 3, 5, and 7 as scoring numbers and 1 as a shift number.

A starts by writing	10
By doubling, B derives	20
By shifting down, A derives	19
By multiplication, B derives	9
By square root, A derives	3 and scores
By shifting down, B derives	2
By doubling, A derives	4

By shifting up, *B* derives —————————— 5 and scores
By squaring, *A* derives ————————————25 and scores
By addition, *B* derives ————————————— 7 and scores
By shifting down, *A* derives ———————————— 6
By doubling, *B* derives ——————————————12
By shifting up, *A* derives —————————————13 and scores
By doubling, *B* derives ——————————————26
By shifting up, *A* derives —————————————27 and scores
By shifting up, *B* derives —————————————28
By halving, *A* derives ——————————————14
By shifting up, *B* derives —————————————15 and scores
By doubling, *A* derives ——————————————30 and scores
By shifting down, *B* derives ———————————29
By addition, *A* derives ———————————————11
By doubling, *B* derives ——————————————22
By shifting up, *A* derives —————————————23 and scores
By shifting up, *B* derives —————————————24
By multiplication, *A* derives ——————————— 8
By doubling, *B* derives ——————————————16
By shifting up, *A* derives —————————————17 and scores
By shifting up, *B* derives —————————————18

No unused number can now be derived (1 and 21 being the only ones remaining) and *A* wins the game by a lopsided score of 7 to 3.

ALEX RANDOLPH CREATES GAMES, at least fifty by present count, with one guiding principle in mind—that each game possess a beauty of its own. This dedication to esthetics has been most successfully translated into game terms as can easily be discovered by trying any of his currently available games: TWIXT (a game of strategically placing barriers), OH-WAH-REE (an updating of the ancient MANCALA that, uniquely, allows for play by three or four), and BREAKTHRU (a different type of war game)—all published by the 3M Company.

Alex now lives in Japan where he is engaged in creating new games, one of which will shortly appear on the Japanese market, and in writing a book on SHOGI, the fascinatingly different Japanese form of CHESS.

In his game of KNIGHT CHASE, Alex makes use of the always intriguing knight's move of CHESS. For those who have forgotten, a knight moves two spaces in one direction and then one space at right angles. In the following diagram, a knight in position A could move to any of the spaces marked B.

KNIGHT CHASE   *by Alexander Randolph*

- *Number of players.* Two.
- *Equipment.* A checkerboard. One black and one white knight from a CHESS set. (If these are not available, checkers can be substituted without altering the game.) Thirty small markers, which may be poker chips, buttons, squares of cardboard, or you name it.
- *The setup.* Each player places his knight in the space at the right end of the row nearest to him. The knights are thus started in opposite corners of the board. The 30 markers are piled, off the board, within reach of both players.
- *The play.* Black always plays first and play then alternates.

A play consists of moving the knight, in a knight's move, to an empty space and then placing two markers. One marker must be placed in the space vacated by the knight. The other can be placed in any empty space the player wishes, except that if only one space is open for the opponent's upcoming move, that space cannot be covered.

Markers, once placed, remain for the duration of the game. When all 30 markers have been placed a turn consists of simply moving the knight.

● *Winning the game.* White wins by moving his knight onto the space occupied by the black knight. Black wins by avoiding capture.

If all 30 markers are placed before there is a capture (Black will place the last 2), White has ten more moves in which to effect the capture and if not successful, loses.

If either knight is blocked so that it, in its turn, cannot move, Black is also the winner.

● *Recording games.* For recording games, the spaces of the board are considered to be numbered as shown in the following diagram, which also shows the starting position of the black and white knights.

11 ●	12	13	14	15	16	17	18
21	22	23	24	25	26	27	28
31	32	33	34	35	36	37	38
41	42	43	44	45	46	47	48
51	52	53	54	55	56	57	58
61	62	63	64	65	66	67	68
71	72	73	74	75	76	77	78
81	82	83	84	85	86	87	88 ○

A player's move is given by three numbers, as 32–11–67. The first number indicates the space to which the knight moves. The other two indicate spaces in which markers are placed. (The location of the first marker does not have to be given but the game is easier to follow if it is.)

● *Sample game number 1*. This shows a quick win by White.

Move	Black	White
1	32–11–67	76–88–13
2	51–32–64	55–76–72

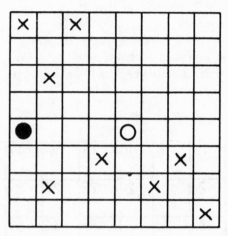

The position is now as shown (X represents a marker) and Black has lost. Whether he moves to 43 or 63, his only possibilities, White is waiting to pounce on him.

● *Sample game number 2*. This a longer game, with Black the victor.

Move	Black	White
1	32–11–76	67–88–13
2	44–32–46	55–67–23
3	52–44–74	34–55–73
4	64–52–53	42–34–56
5	45–64–54	21–42–57

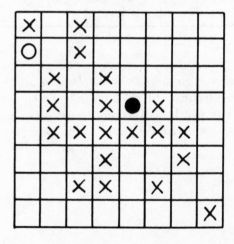

This is the position after the fifth move. Black in his next turn may not place a marker on 33 as this would block White's upcoming move.

6	26–45–25	33–21–47
7	18–26–35	41–33–16
8	37–18–62	– – –

X		X			X		X
X		X		X	X		
	X	X	X	X		●	
O	X		X	X	X	X	
	X	X	X	X	X	X	
	X		X			X	
		X	X		X		
						X	

With all the markers down, the position is as shown. White now has ten moves to try and capture Black.

8	– – –	22
9	58	43
10	66	51
11	58	63
12	66	84
13	87	65
14	66	77
15	78	85
16	86	66
17	65	78

White has not captured Black within ten moves, so Black wins.

JAMES DUNNIGAN is last in this chapter only because I have known him for the least amount of time, just about a year. Jim is at present an aspiring historian, pursuing his chosen field as a student at New York's Columbia University.

A series of published monographs: "Ardennes Offensive," "Battle for France," "Guadalcanal Campaign," and "German Weapons and Tactics in World War II" attracted the attention of the Avalon Hill Company who commissioned Jim to create the game of JUTLAND. This was followed by "1914" and both games, which Jim characterizes as antiwar war games, are currently available.

Jim is also the vice-president of Project Analysis Corporation, which publishes the fascinating magazine *Strategy and Tactics*. Under the auspices of PAC, Jim devised a game, ORIGINS OF WORLD WAR I, which has been used as a learning tool in a number of high schools. From this game an entirely new game was evolved specifically for inclusion in this book. I'll let Jim state in his own words the purpose of the game.

"This is a political-strategy game in which five players represent the five major nations in pre-World War I Europe. They must compete against each other to achieve each nation's 'national objectives.' While actual 'war' is not allowed in the game, the play should show quite clearly how tensions developed to such a high pitch by 1914."

ORIGINS OF WORLD WAR I   *by James Dunnigan*

● *Number of players.* Five.

● *Equipment.* A board as shown in the illustration. This can be as simple, or as elaborate, as desired.

A set of poker chips (fifty white, twenty-five red, and twenty-five blue). If a smaller board is used, cardboard squares (about ½" on a side) will serve in place of chips.

Five cards on which are printed BRITAIN, FRANCE, GERMANY, RUSSIA, and AUSTRIA-HUNGARY (one nation per card).

One die.

● *To start.* Each player chooses a nation and takes the card representing that nation. Or the cards can be shuffled and dealt to the players at random. The players then seat themselves around the able in the following order: Britain, France, Germany, Russia, and Austria-Hungary. Britain will play first followed by the other nations in order.

● *The play.* Each player in each turn places the number of "Political Factors" (PF's) to which he is entitled. (See the board. Britain has

Nations & PF's	Embassies				
BRITAIN 14	(Britain) *	France	Germany	Russia	Austria-Hungary
FRANCE 12	Britain	(France) *	Germany	Russia	Austria-Hungary
GERMANY 16	Britain	France	(Germany) *	Russia	Austria-Hungary
RUSSIA 10	Britain	France	Germany	(Russia) *	Austria-Hungary
AUSTRIA-HUNGARY 10	Britain	France	Germany	Russia	(Austria-Hungary) *
ITALY	Britain	France	Germany	Russia	Austria-Hungary
SERBIA	Britain	France	Germany	Russia	Austria-Hungary
RUMANIA	Britain	France	Germany	Russia	Austria-Hungary
BULGARIA	Britain	France	Germany	Russia	Austria-Hungary
GREECE	Britain	France	Germany	Russia	Austria-Hungary
TURKEY	Britain	France	Germany	Russia	Austria-Hungary
FAR EAST	Britain	France	Germany	Russia	Austria-Hungary
AFRICA	Britain	France	Germany	Russia	Austria-Hungary

fourteen PF's per turn; France twelve; etc. When using poker chips a white chip represents one PF, a red chip represents five PF's, and a blue chip represents ten PF's.)

The PF's are placed in the player's embassies in the nations that he wishes to influence. A player is limited to placing a maximum of five PF's in any one embassy during a turn, but may in subsequent turns add more PF's.

A player may, in order to combat the influence of another nation, place PF's in his own. These are placed in the spaces marked with an asterisk. Any number of PF's can be placed in a player's own nation during a turn (up to the number he is allowed per turn).

● *Diplomatic attacks.* In each turn a player may, if he wishes, make a "diplomatic attack" on a nation whose influence he wishes to reduce. The attack is made after placing his PF's, and a player may not make more than one attack per turn.

In order for an attack to take place the two players involved must have PF's in a common nation, which may be the same as either one of the nations in the conflict or may be different from both. The result of an attack is obtained from the "Diplomatic Attack Table" (next page). To use this table the "odds" are required. These are determined by dividing the total number of PF's that the attacker possesses in the common nation by the total number held by the defender in that nation. If, as is usually the case, the result is a fraction, it is rounded out in favor of the defender.

(For example, Russia has sixteen PF's in its Serbian embassy and Austria-Hungary has eight in its Serbian embassy. If Russia chooses to attack, the odds are 2 to 1. Even if Russia had as many as 23 PF's to Austria-Hungary's 8, the odds would still be 2 to 1.)

If the attacker has less PF's than the defender, the "Less than 1 to 1" column is always used. (In the above example if Austria-Hungary chooses to attack Russia, the odds are "Less than 1 to 1.")

After the odds are determined, the die is thrown and the number matched to the proper column to obtain the result.

(For example, Britain, with twelve PF's in Britain, attacks Germany, who has eight PF's in Britain. The die turns up with a 4. Under the "1 to 1" column "EX" is found. Each nation loses eight PF's and Britain remains with four.)

● *Obtaining treaty rights.* When a nation has ten or more PF's in its embassy in another nation, it has obtained "treaty rights" from that nation. (To make this easy to see, a blue chip is placed on top of the pile of PF's in that embassy.)

74

Diplomatic Attack Table

Die Throw	Odds				
	Less than 1 to 1	1 to 1	2 to 1	3 to 1	4 to 1 or over
1	AE	AE	AE	EX	EX
2	AE	AE	EX	EX	EX
3	AE	EX	EX	EX	EX
4	EX	EX	EX	EX	DE
5	EX	EX	EX	DE	DE
6	EX	DE	DE	DE	DE

AE—(Attacker Eliminated) signifies that all of the attacker's PF's are eliminated, while the defender does not lose any.

EX—(Exchange) signifies that the nation with the lesser number of PF's loses all of them, while the other nation loses an equal amount.

DE—(Defender Eliminated) signifies that all of the defender's PF's are eliminated, while the attacker does not lose any.

If, due to a "diplomatic attack," the PF's are reduced below ten, the "treaty rights" are lost until the PF's are again built up to ten or more.

● *Ending the game.* After all the players have had ten turns the game is ended. The situation at this time is compared with the "national objectives" (Chart p. 77) of each of the five nations and points are awarded to each in accordance with their fulfillment of these objectives.

The player with the most points is the victor. In case of a tie the victory is shared.

● *Making deals.* Players are encouraged to make deals with each other and negotiations can take place at any time during the game. Any type of deal can be made except that PF's cannot be transferred between players and players cannot combine their PF's in a nation in determining the odds for an attack against another player with PF's in that nation.

Players may agree, however, to each attack the same opponent when it is their turn. In this way it is possible to wear down a player with a large number of PF's in a nation and eventually cause him to lose his treaty rights.

Another type of deal is for one player to refrain from interfering with another player's exclusive treaty rights in return for assistance in some other area.

Deals are not enforceable by the rules of the game and any player is free to go back on his word any time that he feels it is to his advantage to do so. The only defense against being taken is to know the reputation of the one you are dealing with or, pragmatically, to "do unto others before they do unto you."

• *Alliances.* Two players, at any time, may form an alliance between their nations. This is a permanent agreement to work together for the duration of the game. (Jim Dunnigan allows a player to back out of an alliance. This, I believe, makes them meaningless.)

Alliances do not change the rules of the game. PF's cannot be transferred between allies or combined in making an attack. If one of the allies can earn points by obtaining treaty right from the other, he must have ten or more PF's in the embassy in order to collect the points.

At the end of the game the points of both allies are added together and if this total is equal to or greater than the combined total of the other three players, the allies have won the game. If not, the highest score among the individual players determines the winner.

It is possible during a game for two different alliances to be formed. Either alliance wins by having at least as many points as the total of the other alliance and the fifth player. In this case the individual player can win with even a low score if he succeeds in bringing about a balance of power between the two alliances. (For example, Britain and France are allied and score 10 points and 11 points respectively for a total of 21. Germany and Austria-Hungary are allied and score 8 points and 16 points respectively for a total of 24. Russia scores 5 points. The 24 points scored by Germany and Austria-Hungary are less than the 26-point total scored by the other alliance plus Russia. Russia therefore ends up the winner.)

• *Play by four or three players.* Although ORIGINS OF WORLD WAR I is definitely best when a full quota of five participate, in a pinch four can play by forming an alliance at the beginning of the game and assigning the alliance to one of the contestants who, of course, plays each nation separately. When only three participants are available, two can be given alliances while the third player handles the remaining nation.

National Objectives

BRITAIN:	Treaty Rights from Italy	3 points
	" " " Greece	1 point
	" " " Turkey	2 points
	" " " Far East (exclusive)	4 points
	No other nation has more than 12 points	10 points
FRANCE:	Treaty Rights from Britain	2 points
	" " " Russia	3 points
	" " " Italy	1 point
	" " " Africa (exclusive)	5 points
	If Germany has not received Treaty Rights from or given Treaty Rights to any nation	10 points
GERMANY:	Treaty Rights from Austria-Hungary	4 points
	" " " Russia	2 points
	" " " Italy	2 points
	" " " Africa	3 points
	If Britain has not received Treaty Rights from or given Treaty Rights to any nation	5 points
AUSTRIA-HUNGARY:	Treaty Rights from Germany	4 points
	" " " Italy	2 points
	" " " Serbia (exclusive)	10 points
	" " " Rumania	2 points
RUSSIA:	Treaty Rights from Serbia	5 points
	" " " Rumania	3 points
	" " " Bulgaria	1 point
	" " " Greece	1 point
	" " " Turkey (exclusive)	5 points
	" " " Far East	3 points

(A nation receives the points for exclusive treaty rights only if no other nation has treaty rights from that nation. For example, if, at the end of the game, Britain is the only nation with treaty rights from the Far East, Britain receives 4 points. If however, any other nation also has treaty rights from the Far East, Britain receives no points for its treaty rights.)

Three

Those PROTEAN PIECES of PIECES of PASTEBOARD

N o GAMING MATERIAL devised by man has proven to be more versatile than the deck of cards. Absolute knowledge as to its invention and spread is not available, and probably never will be, but the earliest known references seem to indicate that the Chinese were using cards in the tenth century A.D. These were numbered cards, divided into four classifications, or suits, and very similar in appearance to the paper money used at that time.

Some three hundred years later a deck of twenty-two picture, or "tarot," cards was developed in Italy. These at first were used for children's instruction, much as the present day game of AUTHORS. Sometime during the fourteenth century the number cards were imported from the Orient and the two concepts were combined to form a new "tarot" deck of seventy-eight cards. This was used in playing the complex trick-taking game of TAROK, a game which still survives in parts of central Europe. Elsewhere the size of the deck has been reduced as the games, in general, tended to become less complicated. The seventy-eight-card "tarot" deck, however, remains as a vehicle for fortune-telling and at present is probably more popular for this purpose than ever before.

Since their inception, thousands of games have been developed to make use of these wonderful pieces of pasteboard. Yet their possibilities, far from being exhausted, seem to be ever expanding. In the two previous chapters five examples of creatively different card games were given. This chapter contains nine of my own invention. Some of these, such as SLAM—a two-hand bidding game—and COLOR GIN—a development from HOLLYWOOD GIN—are conventional in approach. Others, such as OSMOSIS and PATTERNS, investigate entirely new relationships between cards.

80

ALL MY DIAMONDS is a game I conceived as a change of pace from POKER. Although there is no similarity in the play, it satisfies the same urge for speculation. It is basically an auction where players must decide whether they can earn more by buying or by selling.

ALL MY DIAMONDS *by Sid Sackson*

* *Number of players.* Four to seven.
* *The deck.* From a standard deck remove the four tens, leaving forty-eight cards.
* *Preparation.* Chips are used for scoring and a good quantity should be divided equally among the players. White chips have a value of 1, red a value of 5, and blue a value of 10.

At the start of each hand a pool is formed by each player contributing the following value in chips:

If 4 are playing ——15 points
" 5 " " ——12 points
" 6 " " ——10 points
" 7 " " —— 9 points

* *The deal.* Cut for deal, low dealing. The cards are distributed, one at a time, in a clockwise direction, until the deck is exhausted. When five or seven play, some will get more cards than others, but this will be equalized as subsequent deals rotate to the left.
* *Object of play.* The cards are considered to be divided into eight different sets of twelve cards each. Each suit constitutes a set. Also the twelve pictures (K-Q-J), the twelve high cards (9-8-7), the twelve middle cards (6-5-4), and the twelve low cards (3-2-A) each each constitute a set. Thus each column and each row in the following table represents a set.

	◇	♡	♠	♣
Picture	K,Q,J	K,Q,J	K,Q,J	K,Q,J
High	9,8,7	9,8,7	9,8,7	9,8,7
Middle	6,5,4	6,5,4	6,5,4	6,5,4
Low	3,2,A	3,2,A	3,2,A	3,2,A

The primary objective is to win the pool by collecting ten cards from any one of the eight sets. Players, however, can make a profit without winning a pool if they are able to auction their cards for a good price.

• *The play.* Each player in turn, starting with the player to the dealer's left, must auction one or more cards.

The cards auctioned must be a player's entire holding in some set which he announces as he lays them face up on the table. For example, a player holds the following cards: ◊A, ♣2, and ♣3. He could put down all three cards, announcing "All my lows"; or the ♣2 and ♣3, announcing "All my clubs"; or the ◊A, announcing "All my diamonds."

The other players bid for the offered card(s). Bids are made in sequence, starting with the player to the seller's left, and once a player passes, he may not reenter the bidding. The high bidder takes the card(s) into his hand and pays the seller the amount of points bid. The seller must then pay a "tax" to the pool depending on the number of cards auctioned.

If one card is auctioned, the entire selling price goes into the pool. If two cards are auctioned, one half of the selling price goes into the pool. If three cards are auctioned, one third of the selling price goes into the pool. If four cards are auctioned, one fourth of the selling price goes into the pool. And so on. If the selling price does not divide equally, the seller gets the advantage. (For example, a player selling three cards for 8 points would pay only 2 to the pool.)

Each time a player, at his turn to auction, is completely out of cards, he must pay a penalty of 2 points to the pool.

• *Winning the pool.* When a player obtains ten cards from one set he places them face up on the table and collects 60 points from the pool, which is known as winning the first pool. He can only do this immediately after buying a card (or cards) at auction. If he purchases a card (or cards) which gives him a winning set but fails to claim the pool at the time, he must wait until he has made another purchase, though not necessarily from the same set, before being able to win the pool.

The ten cards used for winning the first pool are removed from play and the game then continues as before, with all of the players and maintaining the same sequence of auctions, until a player wins the second pool. The winner of the second pool collects all of the remaining points and ends the hand.

• *Finishing a game.* ALL MY DIAMONDS, like POKER, doesn't have a definite terminating point. As many hands as desired can be played, although it is preferable to finish out a round so that each player has an equal number of deals.

IT WOULD BE DIFFICULT for me to say why, how, or even when I created the following work. Like the game itself, the ideas seemed to flow shapelessly around until, before I realized it, they had taken concrete shape.

OSMOSIS is a subtle game. What constitutes a good hand? What constitutes a good play? The contestants must discover this for themselves, more by intuition than by logic.

OSMOSIS   *by Sid Sackson*

● *Number of players.* Two, three, or four. When two or three play, each plays for himself. When four play it can be either each for himself or as teams, the partners sitting across from each other. Since there are considerable differences between the game for two players and for more than two players, each will be given separately.

The Game for Three or Four
● *The deck.* When four play, use the A, K, Q, J, 10, 9, 8, and 7 from each of the four suits, making thirty-two cards. The Ace is high and the 7 is low.

When three play use the same eight cards from any three of the suits, making twenty-four cards.

● *The deal.* Cut for deal, low dealing. The cards are distributed, one at a time, in a clockwise direction until the deck is exhausted. Each player will have eight cards, which he picks up and holds in his hand.

In subsequent hands the deal rotates to the left.

● *The play.* The player to the left of the dealer plays first. He chooses any card from his hand and places it face up in front of the player to his left. This player "trades" for the card by answering with one of the following:

1. Trading high. Playing a higher card of the same suit.
2. Trading low. Playing the 7 of the same suit. If, however, he holds the 7 and one or more cards of the same suit in sequence with it, he may trade low by showing the sequence and playing the highest card of the sequence.
3. Trading off. If the player can do neither of the above, he must trade off by playing any two cards he wishes, regardless of suit.

(A player who holds cards which will permit a choice between trading high or trading low may choose either. He may not, however, choose to trade off if he is able either to trade high or trade low.)

The two players involved in the trade keep the cards they receive face up in front of them.

The answering player in the first trade now chooses any card from his hand and places it face up in front of the player to his left, starting a new trade. Play continues in this manner with each player in turn trading with his neighbor to the left.

• *Hand cards and table cards.* When starting a trade, a player must play from his hand. When answering, however, he can play from either his hand or from his table cards. If he is trading off he may, if he wishes, play one card from his hand and one from the table.

When a player plays the last card from his hand, he waits until that trade is completed and then picks up all his cards from the table as a new hand.

• *Scoring.* Play is finished when one of the following happens:

1. A player, on picking up his cards from the table, finds that he has four or less cards remaining. This player receives no score. Each of the other players receives 1 point for each card he possesses, whether in his hand or on the table.

2. A player, on picking up his cards from the table, finds that he has eleven or more cards. He scores 1 point for each card he possesses and his opponents receive no score. If it is a four-hand game with partnerships, his partner also scores 1 point for each card he possesses.

When each player is playing for himself, the first to reach a score of 30 or more points is the winner. In case of a tie at 30 or more points, play another hand to break the tie.

When playing with partners, the scores made by each member of a team are combined and the first team to reach 50 or more points is the winner.

• *A sample game.* In a four-player game the initial hands are as follows:

```
                    ♡J  8 7
                    ♣A  10
                A   ◇K  9
                    ♠J

        ♡A K Q                          ♡9
        ♣K 8                            ♣9
    D   ◇Q J                    B   ◇10 8
        ♠8                           ♠A K 10 9
    (Dealer)

                    ♡10
                    ♣Q J 7
                C   ◇A 7
                    ♠Q 7
```

A starts by playing the ♣10. B can neither trade high nor trade low so he trades off the ♡9 and ◇8. A places these two cards face up before him on the table, and B does the same with the ♣10. (Every time a trade is made the cards are left on the table.)

B now plays the ♠9 and C chooses to trade low with the ♠7.

C plays the ♣J and D trades high with the ♣K.

D plays the ♡Q. A shows the ♡7 and ♡8 in his hand and then trades low with the ♡9 from the table. (This comes as somewhat of a shock to D.)

A continues by playing the ♣A. B trades off the ♣9 from his hand and the ♣10 from the table.

The game, of course, goes on, but I will leave it at this point.

The Game for Two

● *The deck.* Use the same twenty-four-card deck as in the game for three.

● *The deal.* Cut for deal, low dealing. Six cards are dealt from the deck and turned face up. These are not used in the play of the hand but are left to one side on the table so that they can be seen by the contestants. The remainder of the deck is dealt out one at a time so that each player has a hand of nine cards.

● *The play.* Play is the same as in the game for three or four, except that if a 7 is included in the six unused cards, a player cannot trade low in that suit. Also, low sequences are limited by the missing cards in a suit. (Thus, if the ♡9 is among the unused cards, the low sequence in hearts cannot be longer than 7–8.)

● *Ending the game.* When a player, on picking up his cards, finds that he has four or less cards remaining, the game is ended and that player has lost.

Each hand is a separate game. If a series of games is played, alternate in dealing.

● *Variation with scoring.* Each player keeps count of the number of times, during the course of the game, that he picks up his table cards to form a new hand. (The twenty-eight cards remaining from the fifty-two-card deck can be used for this purpose. Every time a player picks up, he takes a card and leaves it face down to one side.)

When a player loses (by picking up four or less cards) the other player scores 18 points minus 1 point for each time the loser picked up his table cards, including the last time. However, if a player picks up twelve times without having lost, the hand is considered a draw.

An even number of hands should be chosen and the player with the higher total after these have been played is the winner. Alternate the deal.

• *Duplicate play.* This becomes a test of pure skill for the two players, as each strives to get the most out of the same cards. After the hands have been dealt out, keep a record of the cards. Play the hand and score it in accordance with the above rules. Then reconstruct the hands with each player holding his opponent's previous cards. Play and score the hand a second time. The player with the higher total score is the winner.

PATTERNS has many of the characteristics of a board game. All the cards are face up on the table, so there are no mysteries. Play is in moves, which are determined by the relationship of the cards to one another. Some players find the interplay of the "patterns" a fascinating challenge. Others never see it. To find out whether it is "your cup of tea" you'll have to try it.

PATTERNS is not a difficult game to learn, but the concepts are so different from other card games that it was necessary for me to develop an entirely new terminology. This, of course, will take a little time for the beginner to master.

PATTERNS   *by Sid Sackson*

• *Number of players.* Two.
• *The deck.* From a standard deck of fifty-two cards, one player removes the following twelve cards: ♡A, ♡5, ♡9, ♣2, ♣6, ♣10, ◇3, ◇7, ◇11 (actually the Jack), ♠4, ♠8, and ♠12 (actually the Queen). The other player removes the following twelve cards: ◇A, ◇5, ◇9, ♠2, ♠6, ♠10, ♡3, ♡7, ♡11, ♣4, ♣8, ♣12. The remaining cards are not used. Only the number of the card has any bearing on the play of the game. The suits, however, are a help in seeing the patterns, in much the same way that the alternate coloring on a chessboard makes that game easier to follow.

You will also need twelve chips. Each player takes four and the remaining four form a pool.
• *The setup.* Each player shuffles his twelve cards and deals them face up into a layout consisting of two rows of six cards each, as indicated in the diagram. (The letters are given to identify the position of the cards.)

86

PLAYER X

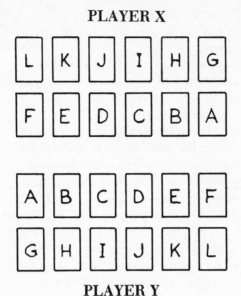

PLAYER Y

• *Object of play.* A player wins by arranging his twelve cards into four sets of three cards each, located in positions A-B-C, D-E-F, G-H-I, and J-K-L.

The numbers in the four sets must correspond to one of the following three patterns:

1. 1-2-3, 4-5-6, 7-8-9, 10-11-12
2. 1-3-5, 2-4-6, 7-9-11, 8-10-12
3. 1-5-9, 2-6-10, 3-7-11, 4-8-12 (This pattern is easy to see since each set is composed of cards of the same suit.)

Any of the four sets of a pattern can be placed in any one of the four locations, and it can run in either direction. A winning arrangement of pattern number (2) might look like this:

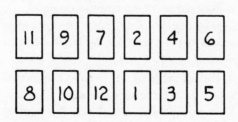

● *The play*. The player who has the higher card at the right end of his bottom row (position L) plays first. In case of a tie, the next card to the left (position K) governs, etc. The player so chosen makes one move. Thereafter each player in turn makes two moves.

Each move consists of switching two cards in a player's layout. (A player may never move his opponent's cards.) Switching can be done in one of the three following ways:

1. *Line Move*. There are six columns of two cards each in a layout. Any two cards in the mover's layout that correspond to such a pair in the opponent's layout can switch position with each other. (Let's clarify this with an example. Looking at the first diagram in the sample game which follows later, we see that player X has an 8 in position A and a 4 in position G. Player Y, as a line move, could switch the position of the 8 and 4 in his own layout.)

2. *Top Move*. If a card in a player's layout is *one* or *two* points higher than either of the opponent's cards in the same column, that card can be switched with any other card in the mover's layout. (Again let us take an example. Player X has a 2 in position E and a 6 in position K. Player Y has a 7 in position B and an 8 in position H. Since the 7 is one point higher than X's 6, Y could switch it with any other card in his own layout as a top move. The 8, which is two points higher than the 6, could similarly be switched.) For purposes of topping, the cards are considered to be in a continuous sequence. Thus 1 will top 12 and 11, and 2 will top 1 and 12.

3. *Neighbor Move*. Any two cards in a player's layout which are next to each other, in a row or in a column, but not diagonally, can be switched. (For example, the 3 in Y's position A could be switched with the 7 in position B or with the 10 in position G as a neighbor move.)

In one turn a player may not switch two cards and then switch them back again, even if he uses two different types of moves.

● *Use of the chips*. Every time that a player makes a line move, he takes one chip from the pool. If the pool is empty, he may still make a line move but does not receive a chip for doing so.

Every time a player makes a neighbor move, he pays one chip to the pool. If he does not have a chip, he is not permitted to make a neighbor move.

Top moves are made without either collecting or paying chips.

If a player wins a hand by using a line move, he collects three chips from the pool (or as many as available if the pool is short). If he wins a hand by using a neighbor move, he must pay three chips to the pool.

● *Scoring.* When a player wins a hand, he receives as many points as he has chips at that time. If he has no chips, the hand is a draw. The number of chips held by the opponent has no bearing on the score.

Play four hands, and the player with the most points is the winner of the game. In case of a tie, play another hand.

● *A sample game.* The cards are dealt out as shown. Each player has four chips and there are four in the pool. (It will be a lot easier to follow the example if the cards are laid out and moved.)

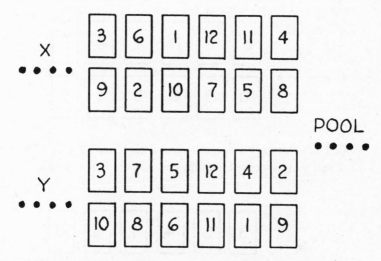

Y, whose 9 is higher than X's 3, plays first. He makes a line move, switching his 11 and 5, and collects a chip. As the first play consists of only one move, his turn is over and the position is now:

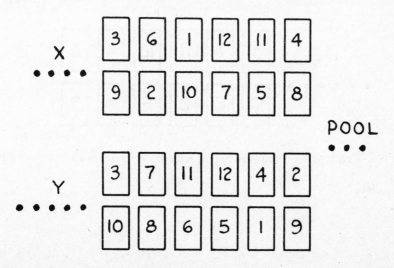

X's 4 tops Y's 2 so he makes a top move, switching his 4 and 10. He then, as his second move, makes a line move, switching his 1 and 4, and collects a chip. The position now looks like this:

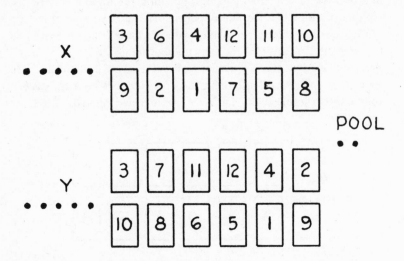

Y's 8, which tops X's 6, is switched with Y's 2. Then as a line move Y's 2 and 6 are switched, earning another chip. The position is now:

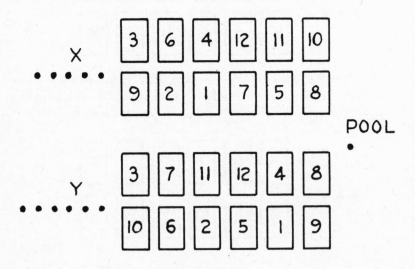

X's 5 tops Y's 4 and is switched with X's 9. The 5 in its new position now tops Y's 3 and is again switched, this time with X's 3, leaving the following position:

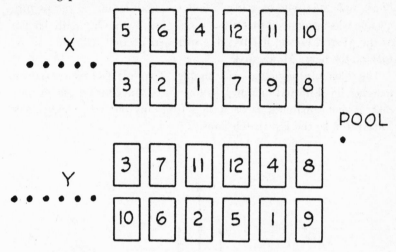

Y switches his 4 and 8. This has to be a neighbor move and he pays one chip for the privilege. Y finishes the game by switching his 1, which tops X's 11, with his 5. The final position is:

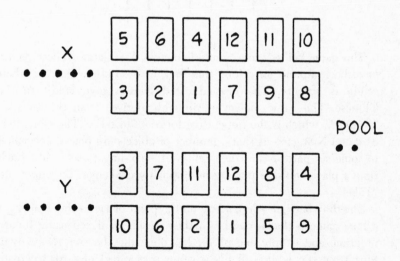

Y's winning position is an arrangement of pattern (3). Y, having 5 chips, scores 5 points.

SEVERAL YEARS AGO a motion picture, *Last Year at Marienbad,* caused considerable controversy between those who took it as a major work of art and those who took it as a monumental put-on. In the picture a game was introduced that also caused quite a stir. Originally known as the MATCH GAME, it later, due to its connection with the movie, took on the name MARIENBAD.

The idea of the game was simple. Two played, using sixteen matches lined up in four rows, as illustrated. In a turn a player may take as many matches as he wishes from any one row. The player forced to take the last match loses.

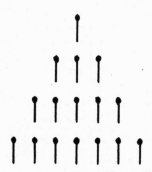

This game belongs to a family known as NIM games. These games have been around for a long time but, as is so often the case, their origin is obscure. The best-educated guesses give credit to the Chinese. The name, however, probably derives from the German *"Nimmt!,"* which is the imperative form of "to take." The characteristic of a NIM game is that a number of objects are placed according to some set pattern and then removed according to set rules. Each time a player finishes playing he implicitly challenges his opponent, "Take!"

The drawback, or—depending on the point of view—the beauty, of a NIM game is that it can be mathematically analyzed using binary notation, and if only one player has done this, he can always win. SUIT YOURSELF, while still a NIM game, uses a deck of cards to create different starting positions for each game so that a player cannot make use of a prior analysis.

SUIT YOURSELF
by Sid Sackson

• *Number of players.* Two, three, or four. When four play it can be each for himself or as partners. With partners, seating should be alternate.

• *Equipment.* A standard deck of fifty-two cards.

• *The setup.* The cards are shuffled and dealt out one at a time into five columns. Two columns will contain eleven cards each and the other three will contain ten cards each. (See illustration below.)

• *The play.* Choose for first in any convenient manner and play then rotates to the left.

Only a card not covered by another can be taken, but as soon as one is taken the one below immediately becomes available.

The first player takes any one card of his choice and places it face down before him. The next player then can take two cards, either from one column or from two. The two cards taken must be of the same suit. The next player can take three cards, from as many columns as he wishes, providing that the three cards are all of the same suit. The next player can similarly take four cards, etc.

As soon as a player takes less cards than he is entitled to under the above rule (as for instance if the third to play takes only two cards), the rule for taking cards changes to that given in the next paragraph. The player must take as many cards as he is entitled to if they are available in the suit he chooses. He may, however, choose a suit in which less cards are available.

After the change, each player in turn can choose whichever suit he wishes and then takes all the cards available in that suit. Play continues until all of the cards have been taken.

• *Winning the game.* Each deal can be considered a separate game and the player with the most cards is the winner.

If desired, a series of five deals can be played and the player with the highest score at the end is the winner. The players score 1 point for each card they take. In addition the player with the most cards in a deal receives a bonus of 10 points. If two players tie for most cards (in a three- or four-hand game), they each receive 5 points. If three tie (in a four-hand game), they each receive 3 points.

• *A sample game.* Let's take a game between two players, X and Y. The cards are dealt out as shown in the illustration. To follow the game you'll have to set up the cards and take them from the layout as stated.

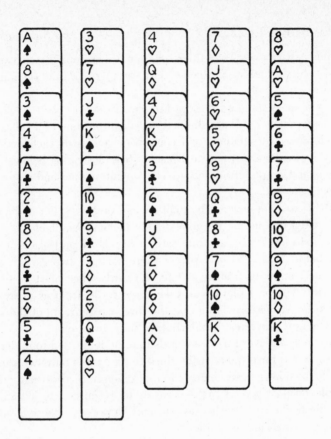

X starts by taking the ♣K from the top of the fifth column.

Y follows by taking the ◇K and the ◇10.

X for his three cards takes the ♠4, ♠10, and ♠7.

Y is entitled to four cards and takes the ◇A, ◇6, ◇2, and ◇J.

X could now take three clubs, but that would permit Y to answer with five hearts. Instead X takes the ♠6 and ♠9. Since X did not take the five cards he was entitled to, the rules for taking now enter the second stage.

Y, for the same reason as X before him, stays away from the clubs and instead takes the ♡Q and ♡10.

X decides to take the ♣5, ♣3, ♣8, and ♣Q. He gets four cards and Y will only get five hearts, a better bargain than on his previous turn.

Y takes the ♡K, ♡9, ♡5, ♡6, ♡J.

X is able to follow up with another five cards, the ◇5, ◇4, ◇Q, ◇7, and ◇9.

Y gets the ♣2, ♣7, and ♣6.

X, to avoid leaving four hearts for Y, takes the ◇8.

Y now takes the ♠2, ♠Q, and ♠5.

X collects the ♡2, ♡4, ♡A, and ♡8.

Y decides to take the ◇3. (Taking the two available clubs would have resulted in his tying instead of winning.)

X takes the ♣A, ♣4, ♣9, and ♣10.

Y cleans up the ♠3, ♠8, ♠A, ♠J, and ♠K.

X is forced to take the ♣J.

Y finishes with ♡7 and ♡3.

Counting the cards that each has captured we find that X has 25 and Y wins with 27.

• *Casino scoring.* Phil Laurence (the creator of PAKS) came up with the idea of using the same scoring system as in the game of CASINO. For those who don't remember, the scoring is as follows:

Most cards ——————————3 points
Most spades ——————1 point
Each Ace ————————1 point
The ◇10 (big casino) ——2 points
The ♠2 (little casino) ——1 point

If cards or spades are tied, nobody scores them. Twenty-five points are game and if there is a tie at or above 25 points, play another deal.

THERE HAVE BEEN THOUSANDS of solitaire or, as they are called in England, patience games published in the last one hundred years. Considering how many have been invented, it is not surprising that some have been tagged with fanciful names, such as PRESIDENT'S CABINET, PANAMA CANAL, WHOLESALE & RETAIL, DIVORCE, PRISON, NARCOTIC, and CASKET, to name a few. The vast majority of these games (although there are a few notable exceptions) are based on stringing cards in sequence, either in the same suit or a red 9 on a black 10.

My idea in creating solitaires has been both to get away from the idea of sequences and to tie the game into a concrete activity.

The name BOWLING SOLITAIRE leaves no doubt as to the activity I had in mind. To enjoy this game it is necessary to keep score as in the parent game, so for those who are not familiar with the scoring I will include a quick rundown.

1	2	3	4	5	6	7	8	9	10
20	46	65	74						

A BOWLING score pad looks something like this. There is room for recording the results of ten "frames." In each frame a player can roll two balls in an attempt to knock down the 10 pins. If all 10 are knocked down with the first ball, the second is not used.

In each frame the player scores as many pins as he knocks down. However, if all 10 are downed, there are extra bonuses as follows.

If a player knocks down all 10 pins in two balls, it is a "spare," which is noted with a / in the upper right-hand corner for that frame. The number of pins downed by the next ball rolled will be added to the 10 pins already scored in the frame.

If a player knocks down all 10 pins with the first ball, it is a "strike," which is noted with a X in the upper right-hand corner for that frame. The number of pins downed by the next two balls rolled will be added to the 10 pins already scored in the frame.

Let's follow the example shown above. In the first frame the player downs 8 pins with the first ball and the remaining 2 with the second ball. The spare is noted in the corner of the first frame. No score is entered yet.

In the second frame he downs 10 pins with the first ball. These 10 are added to the 10 already earned and 20 points are entered for the first frame. The strike is entered in the corner of the second frame.

In the third frame he again downs 10 pins with the first ball. The strike is entered in the corner of the third frame. Scores are not entered yet in either the second or the third frames.

In the fourth frame he downs 6 pins with the first ball. We are now ready to enter the score for the second frame. Ten pins were downed in that frame, 10 were downed by the first succeeding ball, and 6 were downed by the second succeeding ball, making a total of 26 pins scored in the second frame. These are added to the 20 from the first frame to obtain a running total of 46 pins.

With his second ball in the fourth frame the player downs 3 pins. His score for the third frame is 10 plus 6 plus 3, for a total of 19 pins.

96

These are added to the 46 pins to obtain a running total of 65 pins. The score for the fourth frame is 9 pins, the number downed in that frame. These are added to the 65 pins to obtain a running total of 74 pins.

If a player makes a spare or a strike in the tenth frame he throws one or two more balls to determine his bonus.

BOWLING SOLITAIRE   *by Sid Sackson*

* *Number of players.* One.
* *Equipment.* The 10, 9, 8, 7, 6, 5, 4, 3, 2, A of two suits, making a total of twenty cards. Since only the numbers have any bearing on the play, it is preferable to use the two red suits or the two black suits. An Ace is always considered as a 1 and will be noted as a 1 in the description of the game.
* *The setup.* After shuffling the cards, ten are placed face up in a layout representing the ten pins. In the illustration the letters are included to identify the positions. The remaining ten cards are placed in three piles of five, three, and two cards respectively. In a pile only the top card is visible. These piles represent the balls.

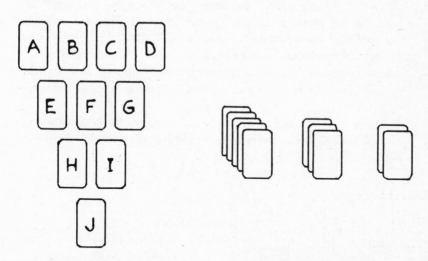

* *The play.* A card from the top of a ball pile can be used for removing one, two, or three cards from the layout. If one card is removed, it must be the same denomination (as a 6 can remove a 6). If two or three cards are removed, they must be adjacent to each other (such as position H-I, or E-F-H, or H-F-G, etc.) and when added

97

together their last digit must be the same as the ball card. (For example, a 6 from a ball pile could be used for removing a 2 and 4, adding up to 6; or a 7 and 9, adding up to 16; or a 1, 2, and 3, adding up to 6; or a 1, 7, and 8, adding up to 16; or an 8, 8, and 10, adding up to 26; etc.) The card from the ball pile and the card(s) from the layout are removed and placed to one side, but the numbers should remain visible as an aid for planning future plays. When a card is removed from a ball pile the one immediately below becomes available.

The first card played from the ball piles cannot be used to remove any card from the back row of pins (A, B, C, or D). The first card also cannot be used to remove the card in position F by itself. After cards have been removed, subsequent plays must have at least one card adjacent to a card already removed. (Thus if cards E and H are removed with the first card from the ball piles, cards C and G could not be removed with the second. Cards F, C, and G, however, could be removed.)

If the player can continue removing cards from the layout until all are gone, he has made a strike. If, however, he reaches the point where no cards from the top of the ball piles can be used or if, in hopes of obtaining a spare, he chooses not to use one that could be used, he has reached the end of the first ball. He now removes one card from the top of each remaining ball pile and places them to one side. With the new cards now available he continues playing. If now successful in removing all the cards from the layout, he has made a spare. If not, he scores as many pins as the cards removed from the layout.

• *A sample frame.* The cards are set up as shown in the illustration. In an actual game the lower cards in the ball piles would, of course, not be exposed.

The player starts by removing the 1 and 9 in positions H and F, using the 10 from the left-hand pile. He would have preferred to remove the 2, 7, and 1 in positions A, B, and C, but is not allowed to take any card from the back row on his first play.

He continues by using the newly exposed 5 to remove the 7, 1, and 7 in positions B, C, and D. (Using the remaining 10 to take the 2, 7, and 1 in positions A, B, and C would have left the other 2 stranded with no possibility of removing it.)

The next play is to remove the 2 and 2 using a 4.

The 5, 8, and 6 in positions G, I, and J now remain. The 8 could be removed, but that would leave an isolated 6 and a 5. Since the second 5 has already been used there would then be no possibility of removing the 5. Instead the player takes a second ball by removing the 8 from the top of the left-hand pile, the 10 from the top of the center pile, and the 4 from the top of the right-hand pile, exhausting that pile.

He now has a choice of two exposed 3s. He chooses (fortunately for him) the one on the left-hand pile and removes the 5 and 8 from the layout.

A 6 is now exposed and the player uses it to remove the remaining 6. He has made a spare.

● *Completing the game.* Ten frames are played, and the object is to get as close as possible to a perfect score of 300 pins.

The game can be played competitively by any number of players. Each one in turn plays a frame and the one with the most pins at the end of the tenth frame is the winner.

LET'S STAY IN A SPORTING VEIN a while longer. BASEBALL has a uniquely interesting play mechanism and, as mentioned before, over a thousand attempts have been made to transfer it to an indoor game. CARD BASEBALL is another such attempt, but quite a few fans have found it to be real BASEBALL lifted bodily from the field and contracted into a deck of cards. It's all there, balls, strikes, sacrifices, steals, pinch hitters, and relief pitchers. And you will need all your managerial know-how to win, because you'll be playing against an opponent, not merely the lucky turn of a card.

CARD BASEBALL
by Sid Sackson

● *Number of players.* Two.

● *Equipment.* A standard deck of fifty-two cards. A rough layout of a diamond on a piece of paper and a few coins will prove helpful in marking the position of the base runners.

● *To start.* Cut, and high card has the choice between batting first or last. Ace is low, counting as 1 throughout the game. The player who has the field first deals six cards to each contestant and you're ready to "play ball."

● *Pitching.* The pitcher winds up and throws one down consisting of any card he thinks best to fool the batter. A picture is a deliberate ball, so the pitcher will usually only lead one when he intends a walk. In any other case he leads a number card (1 to 10) to which the batter replies with a card from his hand. What he plays, of course, determines how well he does. His best bet is to play a card of the same suit as that led. But if he hasn't one or, for some strategic reason, chooses not to play one, he discards any card of another suit and takes a strike.

If the batter throws a card of the same suit, however, he fares much better. If it is a picture, he fouls, which saves him on the third strike at least. If it is a number card lower than that thrown by the pitcher, it is a ball, four of which send him to first base. If it is a higher number card, he connects. But don't start rooting; it isn't a safe hit yet.

Let's take a few examples. Mr. *A*, the pitcher, leads the ♠7. Mr. *B*, the batter, puts on the ♡Q. Strike one!

(Both players, pitcher first, now take a card from the top of the pack, bringing their hands back to six cards. Throughout the game the hand is replenished to six cards every time a card is played. When the deck is exhausted all the cards that have been played are re-shuffled and reused, going through the deck as often as necessary to finish nine innings. Once the game begins the hands are never changed. So play with an eye to the future. Remember, you won't get six new cards at the end of the inning.)

Mr. *A* tries another, the ♠5, on which *B* drops the ♣5. Strike two! *A*, having found a sucker, continues with the ♠8. But this time *B* foul tips with the ♠Q. Still strike two.

A, out of spades, switches style and sends the ♣6. *B* drops the ♣3. Ball one! *A* throws the ♡7 and *B* tops it with the ♡9. It's a hit! But it's far from a safe one because B still has to get the ball past A's fielders.

● *Hitting.* Now that the batter has connected he tries to place the ball where the fielding is weak. He leads any card (don't forget to bring your hand up to six cards first) and the fielder (who is, of course, the same player as the pitcher) responds with one of his own, trying to get as close to the ball as possible. A piece of very simple arithmetic tells you how well the batter fared.

Subtract the lower card from the higher card regardless of whose was lower. (What happens when the batter leads a picture will be explained later. If the fielder is careless enough to have only a picture to play, it is over the fence for a home run.) If the two cards are of unlike colors, multiply the difference by 3; if of the same color but of unlike suits, multiply the difference by 2; and if of the same suit multiply by 1. Then compare the result with the following table and see where the batter lands.

$$0, 1, \text{ or } 2 \text{ ———————— out}$$
$$3 \text{ or } 4 \text{ ———————— single}$$
$$5 \text{ or } 6 \text{ ———————— double}$$
$$7 \text{ or } 8 \text{ ———————— triple}$$
$$9 \text{ or more ——————— home run}$$

Runners on base advance as many bases as the length of the hit.

Let's clarify the above with a few examples. B has just connected with A's pitch. He leads the ♡A and A counters with the ◇2. $2 - 1 = 1$, and then multiply by 2 (same color but different suits). The result is 2 and the batter is out.

Suppose B had led the ◇8 and the best that A could reply with was the ♣6. $8 - 6 = 2$, and then multiply by 3 (different colors). The result is 6 and the batter is safe on second. A runner on second goes home and one on first moves around to third.

And finally, suppose B had led the ♠6 and A had dropped the ◇6. $6 - 6 = 0$ and the batter is out.

● *Calling for a new ball.* In the course of an inning the pitcher's hand is apt to get cluttered with a mass of pictures. Before any pitch he can clean up the situation by calling for a new ball. This is accomplished by discarding two pictures, no more, no less, from his hand, exposing them to the opponent, and replacing them with two cards from the deck. He may pull this deal as often as he wishes, even two or more times in succession, but obviously not between the time a batter has connected and the fielding play is completed. Only the pitcher has the right to call for a new ball.

● *Stealing.* BASEBALL would not be BASEBALL without the opportunity for legal thievery. In CARD BASEBALL the player with men on base and ambition for advancement can act before any pitch. He announces a steal and plays a picture from his hand. If the fielder plays another picture of the same suit, the base runner is caught flat-footed and is out. If the fielder plays a picture of another suit, the runner is sent scurrying back to base. But if the fielder plays a number card, the steal is successful. A player is limited to only one steal try before any one pitch.

Men can be advanced from first to second or from second to third in this manner, but stealing home is another and much more difficult proposition. The play is started in the same way, by the player announcing a steal and leading a picture. But in this case any picture of the same color from the fielder's hand results in an out, and any picture of the other color or any number card of the same suit brings the runner back to base.

For example, *B*, the player who is up, has a man on second base and announces a steal. He leads the ◇K and *A* counters with the ♠J. The runner stays put on second. After a pitch has passed, B tries again with the ◇Q and this time *A* drops the ◇2. The man makes it to third.

A little later in the inning *B* attempts to make it home. He plays the ♣J. *A* answers with the ♣7 and the runner is chased back to third. *B* is persistent and, after a lapse of a pitch, plays the ♡Q. *A* tops it with the ◇J and the man is tagged out somewhere between third and home.

● *Multiple stealing.* A player with two or three men on base can go for multiple larceny. He announces each attempted steal and, specifying which card belongs to which runner, plays one picture card for each steal.

The fielder can choose which attempt he wishes to play to first. That one is handled according to the rules for a single steal.

The other one or two steals have a better chance of success. In stealing second or third, a higher-ranking picture card of the same suit is required for an out, while a lower picture card of the same suit or a picture of the other suit of the same color is required to send the runner back to base. In stealing home, a picture card of the same suit is required for an out, while any other picture card is required to send the runner back to base.

For example, a player has bases loaded and attempts a triple steal. For the runner at third he plays the ♠K, for the one on second the ♦Q, and for the one on first the ♡Q. The fielder plays first to the steal for home and uses the ♣J. The runner is tagged out. To the steal for third he plays the ♦J and the runner is forced back to second. To the steal for second he throws off a ♦5. The runner on first could advance to second except that the base is still occupied and he scurries back to first.

If the third out is made before a runner steals home, the run does not count.

● *Table of steals.* For a quick reference on the above material on stealing, the following table is included which shows the result of the card played by the fielder in respect to that played by the player attempting the steal.

Situation	*Out*	*Returned to base*
Single steal— 2nd or 3rd base	Picture of same suit	Any other picture
Single steal— home	Picture of same color	Picture of other color or number card of same suit
Multiple steal— first runner played to	Same as above	Same as above
Multiple steal; subsequent plays— 2nd or 3rd base	Higher picture of same suit	Any other picture of same color
Multiple steal; subsequent plays— home	Picture of same suit	Any other picture

Any other card is a successful steal, except that in a multiple steal the runner must return if the next base is still occupied.

● *Sacrifices.* The player at bat can also make use of a sacrifice to advance his base runners. A sacrifice is attempted after the batter has

103

connected with the ball. Instead of leading a number card he leads a picture card. If the fielder plays another picture of the same suit, the batter has inopportunely hit into a double play. If the fielder plays a picture of another suit the sacrifice is a success. The batter is out, but the base runner or runners advance one base. If the fielder has no picture card to play, the sacrifice is more than a success. Not only do the base runners advance but the batter is safe at first.

Men can advance from first to second, from second to third, or both at the same time by a sacrifice, but a man on third cannot be sacrificed home.

For example, we will continue with the further adventures of Mr. A and Mr. B. A pitches the ◇6 and B connects with the ◇10. B, with men on first and third decides, with dubious strategy, on a sacrifice. He leads the ♡Q and A puts on the ♣K. B's batter is out but he now has men on second and third. (If a double play had resulted, the batter and the man running from first would be out, while the runner on third would remain.)

In another situation B has men on first and second and again tries a sacrifice. After connecting with A's pitch he leads the ♠Q to which A replies with the ♠J. B's batter is out and also the man running from second to third. B is left, considerably sadder, with two outs and a man on second (who reached there from first).

● *Advanced situations.* With the foregoing under your belt, you are ready to stage a full-fledged game of BASEBALL and get a lot of fun out of it. The remaining seven plays constitute the fine points of the game. You can take them or leave them. But with these added plays every facet of BASEBALL can be reproduced with astounding realism.

The first four situations call for the use of the "companion card," a matter of simple definition. The two cards of the same denomination and the same color are termed companions. Thus the companion card of the ♡7 is the ◇7, and the companion card of the ♠J is the ♣J, etc.

● *Catching a foul.* When the batter fouls by throwing a picture of the same suit on the pitched ball, the fielder can catch the foul, making the out, by playing the companion card.

For example, A pitches the ◇6. B fouls with the ◇Q. If before drawing a card (being an exception to the rule) A has the ♡Q among his five cards, he can play it thereby catching a foul for the out. He now draws two cards to refill his hand.

● *Errors.* When the batter connects with the ball he leads a card, the fielder replies with another, and the two determine how far the batter travels. If the batter can now throw the companion card to that played by the fielder, he causes the latter to make an error. An error allows the batter one more base than he would otherwise be entitled to.

A few more examples will serve to make this clear. B, still up at bat, has a man on third. A pitches the ♠7 and B connects with the ♠9. B now leads the ◊3 and A fields with the ♡4. $4 - 3 = 1, \times 2 = 2$ and the man should be out. But B, without drawing, has the ◊4 among his five cards and plays it. A has now committed an error and B's batter goes to first while the man on third goes home. B must now draw two cards to replenish his hand.

In another situation B has a man on first and then connects with the ball. He leads the ♣8 and A answers with the ◊7. $8 - 7 = 1,$ $\times 3 = 3$ and the man has hit a single. B, however, now plays the ♡7 and A juggles the ball long enough for B's batter to reach second and his base runner to make third.

● *Hit by pitcher.* If, in answer to a pitch of a 10 or a 9 (but no other number), the batter plays the companion card, he has been hit by the pitched ball and goes to first.

● *Double play.* One way of making a double play was discussed in connection with sacrifices, but the fielder has another trick he can pull to produce the multiple outs. When the batter connects with the ball and leads a number card the fielder can, if there is at least one man on base, consummate a double play by throwing the companion card. This does not apply when a sacrifice is attempted.

For example, B, with a man on third, has just connected with A's pitch. He leads the ♣3. A counters with the ♠3 and B has hit into a double play. The batter is out and so is the man on third. If, however, B had had men on first and third, the man on first would have been out, leaving the man on third safe. And if B had had men on first and second, the man running from second to third would have been tagged while the man from first would have reached second safely.

When the bases are loaded it is easier for the fielder to pull a double play. In this case another card of the same denomination results in two outs, while the companion card itself hits the jackpot for a triple play.

For example, B has the bases loaded and connects with the ball. He leads the ♣8. A plays the ◊8 and B is left with two outs, a man on second and third, and a stunned look on his face. If *A* had had the ♠8 it would have been a total blitz, three outs.

● *Long flies.* After connecting, if the batter leads a 10 or a 9, it is considered a drive deep into the outfield. If it is caught, a man on second can advance to third, or a man on third can reach home after the out, provided, of course, it is not the third out.

If the long hit results in a single, a man on second can reach home while a man on first can make third. Finally, if the long hit results in a double, a man can go home from first.

No examples, just for a change.

● *Pinch hitters.* Up to three times in a game each player may substitute a pinch hitter for the man scheduled to come to bat. This is accomplished by the player announcing a pinch hitter and then drawing two extra cards from the top of the deck to simulate the added hitting power of the new batter.

He continues to play with eight cards instead of six in his hand until the pinch hitter has reached a base or has been put out. Then he must immediately reduce his hand to six cards by discarding any excess.

● *Relief pitcher.* Once during the game each player may replace his pitcher with a relief hurler. Before any pitch the player announces the substitution and draws two extra cards from the top of the deck. He plays with eight cards in his hand until the termination of that half of the inning, at which time he discards to reduce to six again.

A player may not make use of a relief pitcher until his opponent has made at least two hits in that half inning. This is to prevent a player from yanking a competent pitcher and putting in the spare hurler simply as a precautionary measure.

EVER SINCE BRIDGE rose to undisputed sovereignty over card games of skill there has been a pressing need for a companion two-hand bidding game of skill; one that would solve the problem of two stranded lovers of the bidding art. Dozens, or probably hundreds, of two-hand BRIDGE variations have been devised, tried, and finally discarded because they could not hold the interest.

The fault of these variations, I believe, has been in slavishly holding to the form of BRIDGE even at the sacrifice of the spirit of the game. Acting on this belief I decided to compile a list of requisites for a really solid bidding game and came up with the following:

1. Bidding must be truly competitive and must be sustained for more than one round.
2. There must be an opportunity for scientific sacrifices, but there must also be apt punishment for a consistent overbidder.
3. The entire deck must be dealt out prior to play of the hand so that strategy can be mapped. However, the play must not degenerate into double dummy by knowing exactly where all the cards are located.

Taking these as a basis and adding some two years of experimentation, I finally developed the game of SLAM. SLAM departs a little from the form of BRIDGE but is successful in keeping the interest and strategy of the parent game.

SLAM offers the beginner an introduction to the fascinating world of BRIDGE and the opportunity to learn without causing anguish to a more advanced partner. And even the advanced player will find that it takes time to master SLAM, but that, after all, is the lure of any skill game.

SLAM   *by Sid Sackson*

● *Number of players.* Two.
● *Equipment.* SLAM is played with a thirty-two card deck formed by removing the 2s to 6s from an ordinary pack. The cards rank A (high), K, Q, J, 10, 9, 8, 7 (low), both in cutting and in play.
● *The deal.* Cut for first deal, high card receiving the nod. In subsequent hands the deal alternates.

The dealer offers the deck for cutting and then delivers ten cards to his opponent and himself, two at a time. A round of bidding follows. Two more cards are dealt to each player followed by a second round of bidding. Another pair of cards is passed out to each, and, with fourteen cards in each hand, the deal is bid to completion. After a trump has been named each contestant receives two more cards, exhausting the deck.

The foregoing is once over lightly on the bidding. Before going into more detail on the choosing of a trump, let's take a look at the play of the hand and the method of scoring. Once this is digested the bidding comes a lot faster.

● *The lay-off and the hand.* The play period begins with each contestant holding sixteen cards, half the pack. Obviously the makeup of the opponent's hand is no mystery. To throw a little darkness on this over-illuminated situation each player now chooses any three cards and places them to one side. The three cards so chosen are designated as the "lay-off," while the remaining thirteen constitute the "hand." The lay-off cards are kept separate and secret until the hand is exhausted, at which time they reenter the game. Experience will show that proper choice of the lay-off is one of the most important, and most difficult, strategies to master in correctly playing SLAM.

● *The play.* With the lay-off taken care of, the defender (player who did not name trump) leads to the first trick. The trick consists of four cards played one at a time, alternating between players. After six of these four card tricks each player is left with one card remaining in his hand. These are played for a seventh trick which, despite its lack of bulk, carries equal weight with its predecessors.

The playing rules are few and simple. The winner of one trick leads to the next. A player must follow the suit led if able; if not, any card can be thrown. The highest card of the suit led captures the trick unless one or more trumps are played, in which case the highest trump wins.

After the hand is played out for seven tricks the lay-off is picked up and continued for an additional three tricks, each consisting of only one card from each player. This makes a total of ten tricks to be fought for in each deal.

● *Value of a contract.* In order to score, the declarer (player who named trump) must take more than half of the ten tricks. The first five tricks won constitute the book. For each trick captured over the book, the declarer scores depending on the trump named. The following table shows the value for each of the possible contracts. (Nullos will be explained shortly.)

No-trump	10 points each
Nullo	10 points each
Spades	8 points each
Hearts	8 points each
Diamonds	6 points each
Clubs	6 points each

As an example, a player names hearts as trump and wins six tricks.

He scores 8 points. Another plays at no-trump and takes nine tricks for a score of 40 points.

● *Nullos.* The player who has a continual affinity for all the low cards in the deck has an out in SLAM. He can play a nullo; nullo being a contract to lose tricks instead of winning them. Mechanics of play are the same as in a no-trump hand, the high card of the suit led winning the trick and the winner leading to the next trick.

Declarer scores 10 points for each trick he loses over the book of five. In counting a nullo hand it is easier to look at the number of tricks that the defender is forced to take. For example, if the defender ends up with eight tricks, the declarer scores 30 points for three over book.

● *The bidding.* With the play of the hand and the point value of the various contracts covered, let's go back to the struggle involved in forcing our pet trump on a protesting opponent. A bid in SLAM consists of a numerical value. If a player intends to play at hearts and is reasonably sure of bringing home eight tricks, he can safely bid as high as 24 points (remembering that eight tricks are three over book and each trick over book at hearts is worth 8 points).

Bidding continues according to rules and procedures, which follow shortly, until the highest number of points is reached. The top bidder becomes the declarer and, for the first time, announces his contract; which is either no-trump, nullo, or one of the four suits as trump.

It is not always desirable to get the contract as cheaply as possible, since only the amount bid is credited toward game. Twenty or more points constitute a game and, while it is permissible to reach this in two or more partial scores, it always pays to make it at one shot if at all possible. Once a game is finished the next game is started without carrying over any partial scores from the completed game.

Another incentive for generous bidding is that the bonus for making a small slam of nine tricks or a grand slam of the entire ten can only be scored if the slam is actually bid.

As previously mentioned there are three rounds of bidding, one with ten cards in each hand, one with twelve, and the final round with fourteen. In each round the dealer speaks first. In the first and second each player has just one chance to speak. In the final round bidding is continued until one contestant passes. If a player passes in an earlier round, he is barred from reentering the bidding. His opponent, however, still has the right to one bid in each round and can fulfill this by raising his own previous bid if necessary.

If both players pass in the first round, a new hand is dealt by the next dealer.

The lowest permissible opening bid is 6 points (which represents one trick over book at clubs or diamonds), but any higher value can be opened. All bids after the opening must be at least 1 point, but not more than 5 points, higher than the preceding bid. The one exception to this rule is that if a player is willing to play a slam, small or grand, he may always bid it regardless of how many points he has to jump to reach it.

The maximum permissible bid depends upon the contract played and represents the point value of a grand slam at that contract. At diamonds or clubs this is 30 points, at spades or hearts 40 points, and at no-trump or nullo 50 points.

● *Doubling.* A defender who feels that his opponent has gone too far can double him. The double is announced immediately after the declarer names his contract. The declarer now may pass (which means he will play his contract doubled), redouble if he feels confident, or change to a different contract if his hand warrants. If the last choice is decided upon, the defender can again double and the declarer can again switch contracts, except that he may not return to his original contract.

● *Keeping score.* Score can best be kept in SLAM by using an ordinary BRIDGE pad. Points bid and made toward game are entered below the line. All points made over the amount bid are entered above the line. Honor melds, penalties, and bonuses are also entered above the line.

● *Honor melds.* Honor melds are announced after the last two cards are dealt to each player and the hands contain a full sixteen cards. Honor melds can be scored by either the declarer or the defender.

With a suit as trump, any trump sequence of four or more cards constitutes a meld. A four-card sequence scores 15 points and each additional card increases this by 15 points up to a maximum of 75 for holding the entire eight cards of the trump suit.

In a no-trump hand three Aces score 20 points and holding all four nets 40. In a nullo three 7s count 20 points and four 7s earn 40.

● *Being set.* A player who fails to make his bid is penalized for the number of points he falls short. His opponent multiplies the point deficit, or "set," by the following values and scores the result above the line. If the unsuccessful declarer has not won a game (is not vulnerable), the multiplier is 3 if the contract was not doubled, 10 if doubled, and 20 if redoubled. For a declarer who has won a game (is vulnerable), the multipliers are raised to 5, 15, and 30.

For example, a declarer bids 20 points, names hearts as his trump, and captures only seven of the tricks. The 16 earned points are 4 short of the 20 bid. If not vulnerable and undoubled, the penalty is only 12 (4 × 3). But a vulnerable and doubled penalty jumps to 60 (4 × 15).

When the declarer fails even to make five tricks for book, the basic value at the contract played of each trick under five is added to the amount bid in determining the "set." For example, a bid of 15, played at diamonds, and netting only three tricks would be figured as 15 plus 2 × 6 for a total set of 27 points, which is then multiplied by the proper factor.

● *Making a doubled contract.* The declarer who is successful in fulfilling a doubled contract, however, profits in two ways. All his earned points are doubled and the entire amount is entered below the line toward game. In addition he receives a bonus, scored above the line, of 25 points if not vulnerable or 40 points if vulnerable.

Redoubling by the declarer serves to double all the above values.

● *Slam bonuses.* Slam bonuses can be scored only by the declarer who bids the point value of the slam he makes. Small slams of nine tricks are rewarded with a bonus of 100 points if the declarer is not vulnerable and 150 points if vulnerable. Grand slams of ten tricks score 200 and 300 points respectively.

● *Scoring games and rubbers.* Twenty or more points below the line constitute a game. When a game is completed, a line is drawn on the score pad and no partial scores are carried over to the next game.

The first player to win two games completes the rubber and earns a bonus of 150 points if his opponent has not won a game, or 100 points if his opponent has captured one.

At this time all the points of each player, both above and below the line, are totalled and the player with the most points, and not necessarily the one to receive the rubber bonus, is considered to be the winner of the rubber.

If a contestant should find it necessary to duck out before the normal completion of a rubber, he doesn't wreck the works. Just wait until the end of the hand, award 60 points to a player who may be ahead one game to nothing, award 10 points to any player with a partial toward game, and settle up the unfinished rubber.

Scoring table for handy reference:

20 Points Are Game.

Value of Each Trick Over 5

No-trump or nullo	10 points
Spades or hearts	8 points
Diamonds or clubs	6 points

Doubled: × 2   Redoubled: × 4

Rubber Bonuses

2-game rubber	150 points
3-game rubber	100 points
Game, unfinished rubber	60 points
Partial, unfinished rubber	10 points

Slam Bonuses

Small—not vulnerable	100 points
Small—vulnerable	150 points
Grand—not vulnerable	200 points
Grand—vulnerable	300 points

Making Doubled Contract Bonus

Not vulnerable	25 points
Vulnerable	40 points

Redoubled: × 2

Set Penalties

Not vulnerable	3 × set
Not vulnerable—doubled	10 × set
Not vulnerable—redoubled	20 × set
Vulnerable	5 × set
Vulnerable—doubled	15 × set
Vulnerable—redoubled	30 × set

Honor Melds

No-trump	4 Aces—40 points; 3 Aces—20 points.
Nullo	4 7s —40 points; 3 7s —20 points.

Suit contracts: Trump sequence of
   4—15 points; 5—30 points; 6—45 points;
   7—60 points; 8—75 points.

• *First sample hand.* To illustrate the foregoing information let's follow the beginnings of a rubber between, let us say, Mr. Jones and Mr. Smith.

They both cut a card and when Jones comes up with a King as against Smith's 10, he deals. Jones deals the cards out two at a time until each has ten. When they sort their cards they find the following hands.

Jones	Smith
♠ J,10,7	♠ Q,9
♡ Q,J,9	♡ K,10
◇ K	◇ Q,10,9,7
♣ Q,10,9	♣ A,7

Jones opens with a minimum bid of 6. Smith keeps the bidding low by raising to 8. This completes the first round of bidding.

Jones passes out another two cards to each and picks up the ♠A and the ♣8, while Smith finds the ◇A and the ♡8. Jones stays low with a raise to 9. Smith, however, sees a chance of making game and raises the maximum 5 points which brings the bidding to 14. This completes the second round of bidding.

Jones gives another two cards to each and Jones receives the ◇J and the ♣K, while Smith draws the ♣J and the ♡A. Their hands now shape up as follows:

Jones	Smith
♠ A,J,10,7	♠ Q,9
♡ Q,J,9	♡ A,K,10,8
◇ K,J	◇ A,Q,10,9,7
♣ K,Q,10,9,8	♣ A,J,7

Jones, seeing he has the weaker hand, passes. Smith is now caught short. The maximum raise of 5 would leave him at 19, just short of game. He decides to take a gamble on a small slam at diamonds and bids 24. Since Jones has already passed, this is the final bid. Now Smith, for the first time, declares his choice of trump, diamonds.

Jones, with the ♠A and ◇K, doubles. Smith considers changing to hearts as trump. Twenty-four points at hearts does not represent a slam, however, and since he jumped to a slam he cannot make the switch. He passes.

Jones now gives out the last two cards to each player and the final hands are as follows (underlined cards represent the lay-off hand):

Jones	Smith
♠ A,K,J,10,8,7	♠ Q,9
♡ Q,J,9	♡ A,K,10,8,7
◇ K,J	◇ A,Q,10,9,8,7
♣ K,Q,10,9,8	♣ A,J,7

Smith, having a sequence of four trumps, the 7 to 10 of diamonds, declares them and scores 15 points above the line.

With the meld taken care of Jones now decides upon the ♠A, ♢K, and ♢J as his three lay-off cards, while Smith picks the ♠Q, ♢A, and ♢Q. These are kept secret and put to one side for later play.

Jones, as defender, leads the ♠8 to the first trick. Smith covers with the ♠9. Jones puts on the ♠K and Smith trumps with the ♢10, taking the trick. Smith now leads the ♢8, Jones throws off the ♠7, Smith puts on the ♢9, and Jones the ♠10. The third trick of the ♡10, ♡9, ♡A, and ♡J also goes to Smith.

To the fourth trick Smith leads the ♡8, Jones drops the ♡Q, Smith covers with the ♡K, and Jones puts on the ♣8. Smith leads the good ♡7 to the fifth trick, Jones puts on the ♣9. Smith throws off his ♣7 loser, and Jones finishes with the ♠J. The sixth trick consists of the J, 10, A, and Q of clubs. And the seventh trick goes to Smith also with the ♢7 taking the ♣K.

Both players pick up their lay-off cards and Smith plays the ♠Q which is taken by Jones' ♠A. (In the play of the lay-off one card from each contestant constitutes a trick.) Now Jones must lead and whichever card he chooses, Smith must win the last two tricks.

Smith has taken nine tricks, four over book, which earns him 24 points, equal to his bid. He scores 48 points (because of the double) below the line. Above the line he scores 25 points for making a doubled contract plus 100 points for bidding and making a small slam.

● *Second sample hand.* After each hand the deal alternates so that Smith deals for the second hand. The ten cards picked up by each player are as follows:

Smith	*Jones*
♠K,8	♠J,9,7
♡A,J,9,7	♡8
♢Q,10,9	♢J,8,7
♣K	♣A,10,7

Smith opens with a bid of 6 and Jones raises to 10, which finishes the first round of bidding.

Smith passes out two more cards to each and picks up the ♢K and ♡10 himself, while Jones receives the ♠Q and ♡Q. Smith bids a minimum 11. Jones keeps game within reach by raising to 15, completing the second round of bidding. The next cards Smith deals to himself are the ♡K and the ♣9; Jones pulls in the ♣J and ♠10. The hands now shape up as follows:

Smith	Jones
♠ K,8	♠ Q,J,10,9,7
♡ A,K,J,10,9,7	♡ Q,8
◊ K,Q,10,9	◊ J,8,7
♣ K,9	♣ A,J,10,7

Smith, intending to play with hearts as trump, raises the bid to 16. Jones, with nullo in mind, bids 20. Smith goes on to 24, representing eight tricks at hearts. Jones, intent on taking the bid, goes to 25 and Smith passes. Jones now announces play of a nullo. No double is forthcoming from Smith and the final two cards are dealt to each player. Smith receives the ♠A and ♣Q, while Jones gets the ◊A and ♣8 completing the hands as follows:

Smith	Jones
♠ A,K,8	♠ Q,J,10,9,7
♡ A,K,J,10,9,7	♡ Q,8
◊ K,Q,10,9	◊ A,J,8,7
♣ K,Q,9	♣ A,J,10,8,7

Jones declares a meld of three 7s and scores 20 points above the line. He then chooses the ♡Q, ◊A, and ◊J as his lay-off cards. Smith chooses the ♠A, ♠K, and ♣9 as his lay-off.

Smith leads out the ♣K to the first trick. Jones puts on the ♣7, Smith the ♣Q, and Jones finishes with the ♣J. Smith then leads the ◊9 to the second trick. The ◊7 goes on, followed by the ◊10 and the ◊8. The third trick also goes to Smith and consists of the ♡7, ♡8, ♡A, and the ♠Q.

To the fourth trick Smith leads the ♠8, Jones goes on with the ♠7, Smith throws off the ◊Q, and Jones takes the trick with the ♠9.

Jones now leads the ♣8 to the fifth trick on which Smith throws off the ◊K, followed by Jones' ♣10 and Smith's ♡K. The sixth trick of the ♠10, ♡J, ♠J, and ♡10 also goes to Jones. And the seventh trick of the ♣A and the ♡9 is Jones' too.

In the lay-off Jones also can't get rid of the lead and takes the final three tricks.

Jones has succeeded in losing only three tricks, two under book. Adding 20 points for two tricks at nullo to the 25 points bid gives a set of 45 points. Since Jones is neither vulnerable nor doubled, the multiplier is 3, making 135 points which Smith scores above the line.

POKER is another game which could use a variation playable by two, and ,very preferably, one that is interesting enough to play without a money incentive. POKE is my answer. When it was published in *Esquire Magazine* back in 1946 it certainly didn't set the world on fire. But, if several hundred letters were any indication, people were playing and enjoying it.

One letter, from a patient in a veterans' hospital, ended by thanking me for having invented POKE. Occasionally, when I find myself doubting whether the creation of another game is worth all the effort involved, the thought of this letter assures me that indeed it is.

POKER is just about the most American of all card games. Yet its antecedents stretch back as far as Persia where a similar game called As or As NAS was played with a twenty-card deck. It spread through Europe where it became POCHEN in Germany and POQUE in France.

The game was most probably introduced to the United States through New Orleans at the beginning of the nineteenth century. By 1837, the full deck of fifty-two cards was being used and American POKER was born. The name itself developed from the French POQUE which was drawled into.two syllables by southern devotees of the new game.

POKE   *by Sid Sackson*

This is strictly a game for two players, using a standard deck of fifty-two cards. Cut for first deal and alternate in subsequent hands.

Each hand is divided into two stages, the first in which the players draw to improve their POKER hand, and the second in which the cards are played out in the form of tricks.

Five cards are dealt to each player. The nondealer starts by either standing pat or discarding from one to three cards and replacing them from the deck. By doing the latter he "doubles" himself; that is, he is penalized double for each trick he loses in the play-out period. If still not satisfied he may discard and draw a second time. This "redoubles" him and he loses quadruple for each lost trick.

The dealer has the option of one free draw of from one to three cards. He may follow this with a double and redouble, making three possible draws in all.

After both players complete their hands, the second stage begins with a lead by the nondealer. A trick consists of one card from each player. High card takes the trick regardless of suit and there is no obligation to follow suit. In case of two equal cards being played to the same trick, the first led wins. The winner of one trick leads to the next. Each player keeps his own card and faces it up to indicate a trick won, or down to indicate a trick lost.

A player may lead to two tricks by playing a pair. The opponent can only win the tricks by answering with a larger pair. If he has a smaller pair, he is not compelled to play it and may discard any two cards. In the same manner three or four of a kind can be played.

Score is kept, similar to SLAM and BRIDGE, in columns divided in the middle by a heavy line. Trick scores are marked below the line, while honors and bonuses are entered above the line.

A player gets 1 point for each trick he takes if the opponent is not under penalty. If the opponent is doubled, each trick is worth 2 points and if redoubled, 4 points.

After the play of the cards the player with the winning POKER hand, in accordance with official POKER rules, receives an honor score as found in the table below. Note that both players may get trick points in the same hand, but only one player may get an honor score.

There is a bonus of 250 points for a player who wins all five tricks in a hand. This is known as a "sweep."

Twenty points below the line constitute a game. With a tie at 20 or more points, play another hand to break the tie. The player making game gets a bonus of 100 points above the line and all partial scores of the opponent below the line are canceled. When a player wins his second game he gets the 100-point game bonus in addition to a rubber bonus of 750 points if opponent has not won a game, or 500 points if opponent has won a game. When a rubber is completed, the player with the highest score above the line is the winner.

Table of Honor Values

Pair	50 points
Two Pair	100 points
Three of a Kind	200 points
Straight	300 points
Flush	400 points
Full House	500 points
Four of a Kind	600 points
Straight Flush	750 points
Royal Flush	1000 points

Table of Bonus Values

Game Bonus	100 points
2-Game Rubber Bonus	750 points
3-Game Rubber Bonus	500 points
Sweep Bonus	250 points

● *Sample hand.* For illustrative purposes let's take a hand played between Mr. A and Mr. B. A deals and B gets ♠Q, ♡Q, ♡3, ♣3 and ◇4, while A comes up with ◇10, ♡6, ♡4, ◇3, and ♣2 himself.

Opening move goes to B, who fishes for a full house by discarding the ◇4, doubling himself. He draws ♠8 and lets the matter stand.

A has possibilities for a straight but skips them in favor of improving the strength of his hand. A low straight, although worth 300 points in honors, is wide open to a sweep by the opponent. He discards ♡4, ◇3, and ♣2 and replaces them with ♠10, ♡K, and ♣5. For a "double" he keeps only the pair of 10s, but draws three more low cards. For a "redouble" he discards these and draws ♡10, ♣K, and ◇5, bringing his hand up to three of a kind.

B opens with his pair of Queens and A throws off ◇5 and ♡10. B next leads the pair of 3s which A tops with his remaining two 10s. The last trick is A's, with his ♣K beating B's ♠8.

Below the line B scores for two tricks at 4 points each, for a total of 8 points. A scores three tricks at 2 each, for a total of 6 points. A also scores 200 points above the line for three of a kind.

If A had stopped after his free draw, he could have won the same number of tricks and B would have made only 2 points below the line. But instead of A's scoring 200 honors, B would have scored 100, a total gain of 300 for B. Which was the more worthwhile depends entirely upon the score at the start of the hand.

● POKE *with deuces wild.* For those who long for big hands and plenty of them, I suggest playing with deuces wild. The rules are the same as for regulation POKE except that a 2 can be used as any other card. The deuce must represent the same card in both the play-out period and the scoring for honors. To make up for the higher honor values that will result, double the bonus values. Game bonus becomes 200, sweep bonus becomes 500, and rubber bonuses become 1500 and 1000.

With deuces wild, five of a kind is possible and this scores 1000 points in honors or equal to a royal flush.

● BLUFF POKE. In this variation, devised for inveterate gamblers, a round of betting is introduced at the close of the drawing period and before the play-out. Nondealer may open with a bet of "double honors." Dealer has the choice of refusing the bet, seeing it, or raising it. If the dealer chooses to refuse the bet, nondealer collects the honor score for his, nondealer's, hand even if it is lower than that of the dealer.

If dealer sees the bet, the winning POKER hand will score twice the regular number of points. If dealer wishes to raise, he calls for "triple honors." Nondealer may back out, in which case dealer gets double the honor score even if his hand is lower. Nondealer may also see the bet or raise it to "quadruple honors," which is the highest possible bet.

If nondealer originally passes, dealer may open the betting with "double honors."

In this variation, as in the preceding one, the bonus values are doubled. If BLUFF POKE is played with deuces wild, the bonus values are quadrupled. Game bonus becomes 400; sweep bonus becomes 1000, rubber bonuses become 3000 and 2000.

● HANDICAP POKE. In this variation the trailing player is given a handicap in the form of the chance to deal. If neither contestant has won a game, or if both have won games, the one with the lower score below the line deals. If the trick score is even, the one trailing above the line deals. If absolutely even, cut for deal.

When only one player has won a game, the opponent keeps the deal until either the rubber is won or the games are evened at one to one.

THERE WAS, OF COURSE, no need for me to come up with a two-hand RUMMY game. GIN RUMMY already is, as mentioned before, the most popular two-hand card game around. For the GIN fan, however, who is fascinated by HOLLYWOOD and its three games at one time, I devised COLOR GIN, which goes one step further and gives the player four games at a time. But the difference is more than simply a matter of numbers. In COLOR GIN each game is a distinct game and the player must consider in his strategy just how many he is aiming to score in.

RUMMY, incidentally, can also be traced back to the Chinese. MAH JONG, which is basically a game of forming groups of three of a kind (pungs), groups of four of a kind (kongs), or sequences of three of the same suit (chows), has been played in China for many centuries. Introduced to this country during the 1920s, it has undergone considerable change (for the worse in my opinion) which has obscured its fundamental identity with RUMMY.

COLOR GIN   *by Sid Sackson*

Two play, using a standard deck of fifty-two cards and a score pad drawn up as follows.

♠		♡		◇		♣	
YOU	ME	YOU	ME	YOU	ME	YOU	ME

As you can see, a separate game is played in each suit. The rules of GIN are followed in all cases, but you must bear in mind that you are trying to score in as many suits as possible.

An unmatched card or a sequence stop you from scoring in that suit. You also do not score in the missing suit if you have three of a kind.

A few examples will make this clear. Suppose I knock with the following hand: ♠10, ♡10, ◇10; ♠7, ♠6, ♠5, ♠4, ♠3; ◇3, ◇A and you are caught with 15 points. It is clear that I win 11 points, but we have to check to see in which suits. I am lacking the ♣10 so my hand is spoiled in clubs. I have a sequence in spades which kills that suit. And the two unmatched diamonds ruin me in diamonds. I record 11 points only in the heart game.

Next hand you go gin with the following:
♠Q, ♣Q, ♡Q; ◇Q, ◇J, ◇10; ◇6, ◇5, ◇4, ◇3 and I'm stuck with 18 points. In your Queen meld you are lacking the ◇Q and both of your sequences are in diamonds, so your hand is spoiled only in that

120

suit. You score 38 points (18 points plus 20 points gin bonus—the bonus values can be varied in accordance with the preferences of the players) in the club, heart, and spade games.

In the third hand you knock with ♠J, ♢J, ♡J, ♣J; ♠9, ♠8, ♠7, ♠6; ♣4, ♠2 and I can reduce my count to zero points. Your hand is spoiled in spades by the sequence and the unmatched card and in clubs by the unmatched card. If you had won, you would have scored in diamonds and hearts. Since you were set, I score 16 points (6 points plus 10 points undercut bonus) in the same suits, diamonds and hearts.

At the end of the third hand the score pad will look like this.

♠		♡		♢		♣	
YOU	ME	YOU	ME	YOU	ME	YOU	ME
38		38	11		16	38	
			27				

You cannot knock or go gin unless you can score in at least one game. When 100 points (or a different amount if preferred by the players) are reached in a suit, that game is completed and there is no further scoring in that suit. When play has been reduced to only one or two suits you must be careful to keep your hand good in a remaining suit or you may find yourself in the frustrating position of having a beautiful gin hand and not being able to do a thing with it.

Four

New
BATTLES
on an Old
BATTLEFIELD

E VER SINCE THE SEVENTH CENTURY, with the invention in India of a primitive form of CHESS, make-believe wars have been conducted on a board divided into sixty-four squares. Even prior to that, a board of the same size was used for playing ASHTAPADA, a race game which is a direct ancestor of our present day PARCHEESI. On this board certain squares were crosscut and the modern Indian chessboard still contains many of these markings, even though they have long since lost their significance.

The complete rules for ASHTAPADA have been lost, but it is known that men were entered in the marked squares in the middle of the outside line and then traveled along prescribed paths until they reached the center of the board. Crosscut squares were also safety spaces where pieces were not subject to capture.

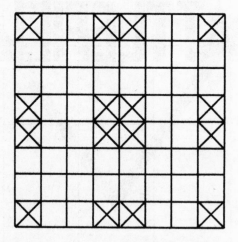

THE ASHTAPADA BOARD

The chessboard became the checkerboard during the thirteenth century with the introduction of alternate coloring of the spaces. And by the beginning of the fourteenth century the game we now know as CHECKERS was becoming popular throughout Europe.

Although other games, notably FOX AND GEESE and REVERSI, are played on the board, to the vast majority only CHESS and CHECKERS are familiar. To remedy this, three fresh approaches were presented in Chapter Two and this chapter will present another three that I have created: FOCUS, NETWORK, and TAKE IT AWAY.

FOCUS is already familiar to readers of Martin Gardner's column in *Scientific American Magazine,* where the two-hand version was presented in the October 1963 issue. Commenting letters indicated a following around the United States and in several foreign countries. Polish game fans were later introduced to FOCUS through Lech Pijanowski's Warsaw newspaper column.

FOCUS is not CHESS, or CHECKERS, or a cross between them. It is a new game with a flavor, a feeling, and a method all its own.

FOCUS is much easier to learn than CHESS. All the rules can be learned in five minutes. Mastery of the strategy can take a lifetime; but who would want it otherwise?

FOCUS is a fast-moving game. Contact between the forces is immediate. And at the end of the game a small superiority in power can bring about a speedy conclusion. While a draw is a theoretical possibility, after hundreds of games I have yet to encounter one.

FOCUS, unlike CHESS or CHECKERS, lends itself naturally to play by four. On the same board as that used for the two-hand game, a partnership version is played which some fans find to be even more challenging.

FOCUS *by Sid Sackson*

• *Number of players.* Two or four.

• *Equipment.* For playing FOCUS you will need a checkerboard with the four corners missing as shown in Illustrations 1 and 6. This can be easily accomplished by pasting a piece of paper over the squares to be masked. To those who would like to try the game before plunging, just go ahead on the full checkerboard—it is almost the same game.

For two players you will need checkers of two colors, 18 for each. Two regulation sets will take care of this. Those with interlocking edges work best.

For four players you will need checkers of four colors, 13 for each. Finding matching checkers of four colors can be a problem, one solution being to paint your own, using paints sold for the coloring of plastic models.

As an excellent substitute for checkers, it is possible to use poker chips; again the interlocking type are best. Small chips in a wide variety of colors are available.

(An attractive, inexpensive Focus set is put out by the Whitman Publishing Company.)

The Game for Two

The game will first be explained for two players. Then additional rules for four will be given.

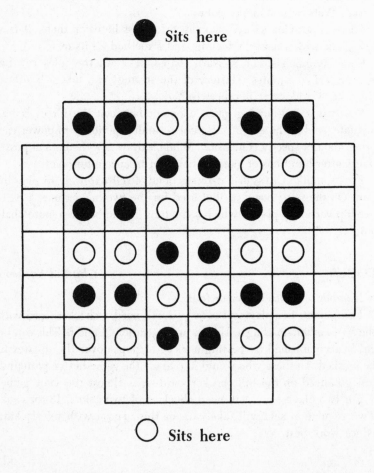

Illustration 1   Starting position—   2 players

• *To start.* The pieces are put down at the start as shown in Illustration 1. To choose the player who moves first, one of the players holds a black piece in one fist and a white one in the other. The second contestant picks a fist and the color chosen plays first.

• *The moves.* A move consists of moving a pile of pieces as many spaces as there are pieces in the pile. A move is made in one straight line and can be up, down, to the right, or to the left, but never diagonal.

At the beginning of the game all piles are 1-high, so only one space can be moved. Illustration 2 shows the possible moves of a piece at the start of the game.

Illustration 2

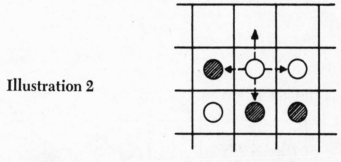

By moving up (in Illustration 2), the white piece lands on an empty space. By moving to the right, it lands on a white piece forming a 2-high pile. By moving to left or down, it lands on a black piece, also forming a 2-high pile, which is controlled by the white player since a white piece is on top.

A 2-high pile can be moved two spaces, as indicated in Illustration 3.

Illustration 3

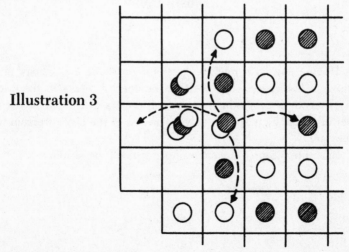

Three-high, 4-high, and 5-high piles can similarly be moved three, four, and five spaces.

A pile can be moved over an intervening space whether it is empty or occupied by a pile controlled by either player. The piles passed over are not affected in any way. A move may end either on a pile or on an empty space.

● *Captures and reserves.* Piles can be built up to a maximum of 5-high. If a move is made causing a pile to become greater than 5-high all pieces in excess of 5 are removed from the *bottom* of the pile.

Pieces of the opposite color to the player making the move are captured and are out of the game. Pieces of the player's own color go into that player's reserves, from which they can reenter the game.

Illustration 4 presents an example of this type of move.

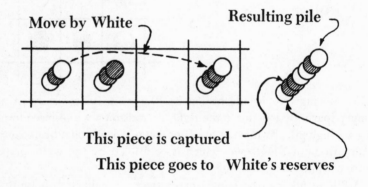

This piece is captured

This piece goes to   White's reserves

Illustration 4

● *Moving part of a pile.* A player in control of a pile may make a move of less spaces than the total number of pieces in the pile. He does this by lifting as many pieces off the *top* of the pile as the number of spaces he wishes to move. The rest of the pieces remain where they are.

Illustration 5 presents an example of this type of move.

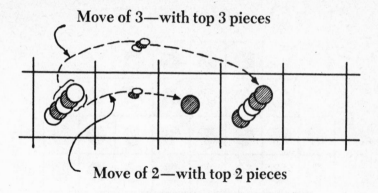

Move of 3—with top 3 pieces

Move of 2—with top 2 pieces

Illustration 5

White (in Illustration 5) may take 3 pieces off the top of his pile, landing on top of the 5-high black pile. The 2-high pile remaining would be controlled by Black. White, however, by this play would gain 1 capture and 2 reserves.

White could instead take 2 pieces from the top of his pile and land on top of the 1-high black pile. The 3-high pile remaining would still be controlled by White.

These, of course, are only two of the possible moves.

● *Playing from reserves.* When a player has reserves he may, on any turn, make use of one of his reserves instead of moving a pile. This is done by taking a piece from his reserves and placing it on any space on the board, whether empty or containing a pile. The effect of this piece is exactly the same as if it had been moved from another position on the board.

● *Winning the game.* When it is a player's turn to move and he controls no piles and he has no remaining reserves (in other words, he cannot make a move) the game is over and his opponent is the winner.

The Game for Four

With four players each one uses 13 pieces which are placed on the board as shown in Illustration 6. (As a variation, 12 pieces of each color can be used. In this case the pieces in spaces 22, 27, 72, and 77 [see Illustration 7] are omitted.)

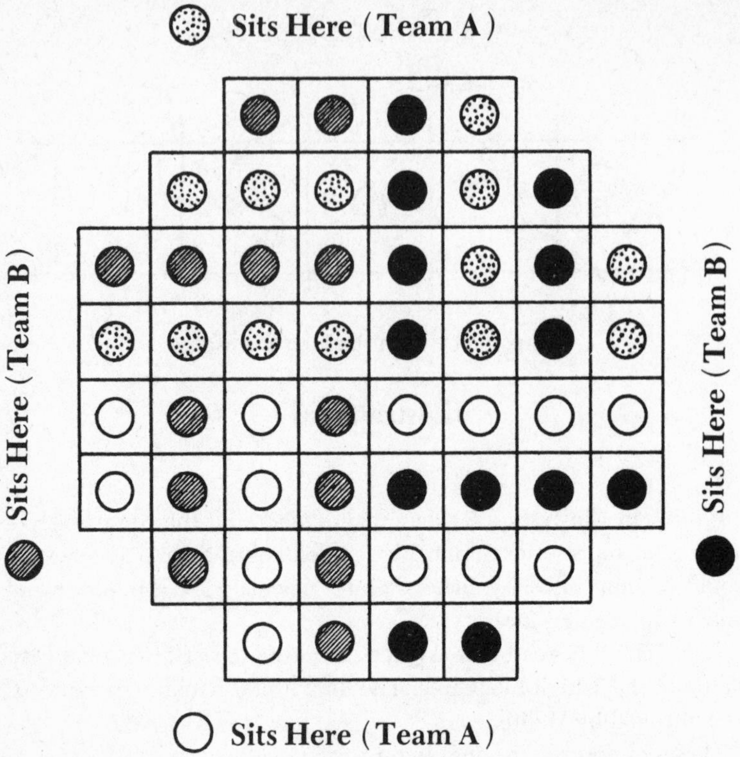

Illustration 6   Starting position— 4 players

The four-hand game is always played with partners. Partners are seated so that they face each other across the board.

To choose the player who moves first, take a piece of each color, mix them together, and draw one blindly. The color chosen makes the first move and play then continues around the board in a clockwise direction.

All rules of two-hand play are used with the following additions:

If a player captures pieces belonging to his partner, instead of removing them from the game he gives them to his partner for his reserves.

A player who is not able to move when it is his turn to play is not out of the game if his partner is still able to move. He simply loses his turn, and continues to do so until either the game is over or it again becomes possible to move. This can happen by his getting reserves from his partner or by the moving of part of a pile, leaving him in control of the remainder.

When both partners of a team are not able to make a move the game is over and the opponents are the victors.

When playing four-hand it is essential to agree whether it will be allowable for the partners to talk about their plans. The best game results when silence is maintained. However, if some of the players are inexperienced, it is preferable to allow for free consultation between the partners. Whatever agreement is made, stick to it. It is not fair for one set of partners to maintain silence while the other set consults.

● *A few playing hints.* Unlike other board games of strategy, in Focus the contact with the enemy is immediate. The first few moves usually consist of moving 1-high piles, forming 2-high piles. Try to line up your 2-high piles so that they focus on one space. When consolidated these will result in captures of the opponent and, of even more importance, reserves for yourself.

In the early stages of the game beware of moving into a space between three, or even two, of opponent's 1-high piles. In fact, at any stage of the game a 1-high pile is a potent threat if it can be moved next to an opponent's higher piles.

Always be on the watch for two large piles facing each other on the same line. In this situation the player who succeeds in getting in the first punch can reap a tremendous advantage.

When you control a large pile don't be afraid to move part of it, leaving your opponent in control of one or two pieces, if you can gain captures or reserves by so doing.

Another occasion for moving part of a pile is when a large pile is under attack by the opponent. Moving part of the pile serves a double purpose. The remaining pile is smaller and less likely to go over 5, and also the part moved off is in position to be moved back to regain control if your opponent attacks.

In the final stages of a game it is often proper strategy not to continue the attack on the opponent, but instead to focus on consolidating your own piles in order to obtain more reserves. With a preponderance of reserves the game can be rapidly terminated.

Reserves are of primary importance at an any stage of the game. Letting the opponent obtain too large a lead in reserves is tantamount to losing the game.

One situation to look for is a 5-high pile controlled by your opponent but with your color on the bottom. By playing a reserve you take over control of the pile and also get back a reserve. Depending on the arrangement of the pile, your opponent may be able to make a similar play! Eventually, however, one player will stop getting back a reserve. Experience will teach you who will finally end up in control.

In partnership play the opportunities for strategic teamwork are endless. One tactic is for both partners to attack the same opponent. Unless his partner is on the alert to help him, he will find himself unable to parry both attacks. It is always important for the player in a strong position to do everything in his power to assist his weaker partner. Otherwise he will find himself ending the game playing two against one.

● *An illustrative game.* The best way to pick up a game is to watch it being played. Readers who will take the time to play through the following two-hand game will find examples of all the moves. Since the game is one that was actually played, the strategy is not perfect and the reader will, no doubt, be able to notice many places where he would play differently.

For purposes of recording a game the board is considered to be numbered as shown in Illustration 7. The pieces are placed to start as shown in Illustration 1.

			13	14	15	16	
		22	23	24	25	26	27
31	32	33	34	35	36	37	38
41	42	43	44	45	46	47	48
51	52	53	54	55	56	57	58
61	62	63	64	65	66	67	68
	72	73	74	75	76	77	
		83	84	85	86		

Illustration 7

A move is recorded by noting the starting square and the finishing square. Plays from reserves are noted by using an R instead of a starting square. Moves that result in captures or reserves are followed by C or R. A move of part of a pile is apparent from the number of spaces moved, but as an added reminder all such moves are underlined.

Black wins the pick for first move.

Move	Black	White	Move	Black	White
1	55-45	44-43	13	46-43R	63-43CR
2	66-65	64-63	14	46-45	43-83
3	35-25	72-62	15	74-73	43-33
4	34-33	53-54	16	75-76	33-63
5	65-45	56-46	17	45-85	67-65
6	42-43	37-47	18	85-83R	63-83CC
7	43-45C	77-67	19	85-83CC	63-73
8	25-45RC	47-45CR	20	R-73	62-42
9	R-45R	R-45R	21	22-32	52-42
10	R-45R	36-46	22	23-24	65-63
11	27-26	46-45C	23	83-33	42-32
12	26-46	45-43	24	73-33RRCC	57-67

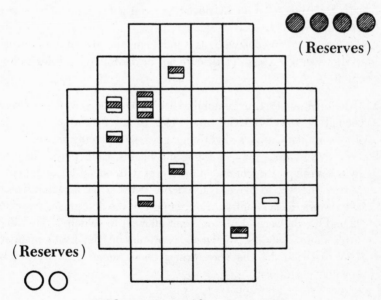

(Reserves)

(Reserves)

The position after move 24

White would normally resign after Black's twenty-fourth move, but to show how reserves are used in terminating a game the remaining moves are included.

Move	Black	White	Move	Black	White
25	R-32	67-77	33	R-63	R-33R
26	32-36	54-52	34	63-33RRC	56-54
27	76-56	77-67	35	R-52	54-52
28	56-36C	67-57	36	R-52R	R-52R
29	R-36R	R-36R	37	R-52R	47-46
30	R-36R	R-36R	38	R-42	46-47
31	R-36R	57-47	39	R-47	R-33C
32	36-33RCR	36-56	40	R-33C	R-33C
			41	R-33C	

Some Final Remarks for Advanced Players

After Focus was printed in *Scientific American Magazine,* several correspondents called my attention to the possibility of the second player imitating the moves of the first player. For example, if Black starts with 54-44, White answers with 45-55. If Black continues with 23-24, White's response is 76-75. And so on. White can continue until he sees a chance to profit by deviating. And if he doesn't, he is still assured a draw.

My answer to someone who plays in this manner, is not to play with him. However, for a less drastic cure one of the following rules can be adopted.

1. If neither player can immobilize the other, the one who played second is considered the loser. This is not too unfair, since in Focus, unlike Chess, a slight edge goes with playing second.
2. Before the actual play of the game begins, each player in turn switches the position of one of his pieces with one of his opponent's pieces. The second player is not permitted to make a switch which will restore the symmetry. (For example, if the first player switches 22 and 64, the second player is not allowed to switch 77 and 35.) After these switches, the game continues in the usual manner. This variation, by the way, brings about some fascinating new opening positions.

FOR QUITE A LONG TIME I have been fascinated with the idea of arranging checkers on a board so that they form a chain, connected to each other along a straight line, but with intervening empty spaces. It provided an interesting way of doodling, but wouldn't coalesce into a game until one simple idea presented itself to me. That was the idea of limiting friendly pieces in a group to a maximum of 2 (which, of course, won't mean much to you until you read the rules.)

With this concept, the game of NETWORK fell into place in a matter of minutes. It is a game of pure strategy, but it is a fast game. It usually averages about ten moves by each contestant, which allows for the playing of a good number of games in a session.

NETWORK   *by Sid Sackson*

* *Number of players.* Two.
* *Equipment.* A checkerboard and 10 checkers for each player.
* *The board.* For purposes of playing the game the board is considered divided into areas as indicated in the diagram (though there is no need to actually mark the board).

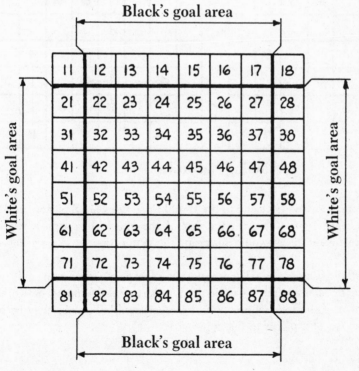

Black's goal areas consist of squares 12, 13, 14, 15, 16, 17 and of 82, 83, 84, 85, 86, 87. Only Black may place pieces in these areas. White's goal areas are 21, 31, 41, 51, 61, 71 and 28, 38, 48, 58, 68, 78 and only White may play here. The corner squares—11, 18, 81, and 88—are dead and neither player may use them.

● *Object of play.* The object of each player is to complete a "network" joining his two goal areas. The network must start at one goal area and terminate at the other and must contain at least 6 pieces which are connected to each other along straight lines, either orthogonal or diagonal.

The following two diagrams show winning networks that Black could fashion from the 9 pieces he has placed on the board. (To make the networks easier to see, the enemy pieces are not included.)

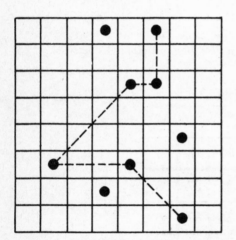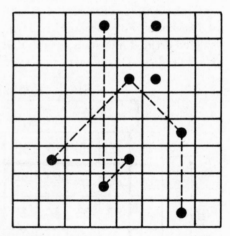

Winning Networks

An enemy piece placed in the straight line between 2 pieces breaks the connection. (Thus, in the first of the above diagrams, a white piece in square 76 would interrupt the connection to Black's lower goal.)

Although more than 1 piece may be placed in a goal area, only 1 piece in each goal area can be used as part of the winning network. Neither of the following networks are permissible because they both make use of 2 pieces in the upper goal.

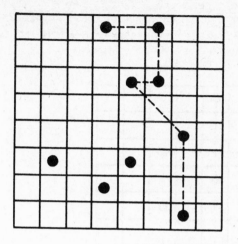 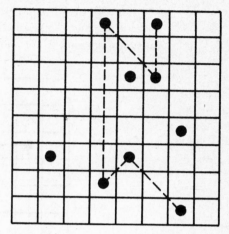

Incorrect Networks

A network may not pass through the same piece twice, even if it is only counted once. For that reason the following network is not valid.

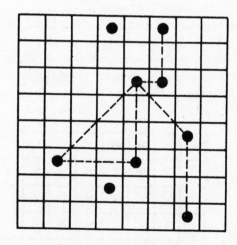

Incorrect Network

A network may not pass through a piece of the player's own color without turning. Consequently, because of the piece in square 44, the following network is not allowable.

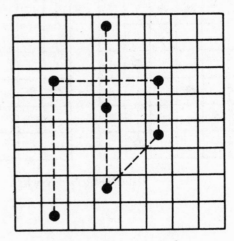

Incorrect Network

● *The play.* Choose for first player in any desired manner and alternate if a series of games is being played.

Each player in turn places 1 piece in a vacant square. A player may not have more than 2 of his pieces in an adjoining group, whether connected orthogonally or diagonally. Thus in the following diagram, Black, with 7 pieces on the board is not permitted to place a piece in any of the squares marked with an X because doing so would form a group of 3 or more pieces. (And he, of course, may not place pieces in White's goal areas or the corner squares.)

• *When all the pieces are placed.* If all of the pieces are placed before the game is won, each player in turn moves any one of his pieces to any vacant square, subject to all previous restrictions, until the game is completed.

A player is not permitted to make a move which will result in both players completing a network. (This could come about by a player removing a piece which blocked a winning network by the opponent and replacing this piece to form a winning network for himself.)

Additional Rules for Advanced Players

• *Announcing threat.* When a player is in a position to win in his next turn, he announces "threat" and points out the direction of the threat, giving the opponent an opportunity to defend against it. (With this rule, as with the checkmate rule in CHESS, a game must be ended by a winning position, rather than by an oversight.)

• *Privilege.* Since NETWORK is a short game, experienced players will find that the first player has a decided advantage. To restore the balance, the following "privilege" is given to the second player.

In placing his pieces, the second player is permitted to form either two groups of 3 pieces each or one group of 4 pieces. However, once all the pieces have been placed and moving begins, the player can no longer avail himself of this "privilege"; all pieces, including one removed from an oversize group, must be put back on the board under the usual restrictions.

• *A sample game.* The following is the record of a hard fought game that was played using the "threat" and "privilege" rules. For the first ten moves only the number of the square occupied is noted. After this, two numbers are required: the square vacated and the square entered. A "T" indicates a threat.

White won the toss for first play.

Move	White	Black	
1	55	53	
2	73	75	
3	66	33	
4	71	77	
5	36T	46	White threatens 71-73-55-66-36- and 38 or 58.
6	35T	47	White threatens 71-73-55-35-36-58.

Move	White	Black
7	63T	72	White has more than a triple threat; either 71-73-63-66-55-58 or 71-73-55-35-36-63-66-48 or 71-73-63-36-35-55- and a few choices from here. Etc.
8	51T	62	The same threat. Black uses his "privilege" to form a group of 3.
9	41T	52	A similar series of threats. Black uses up his "privilege" by forming a group of 4.
10	23	87T	Black threatens 87-77-75-53-33-15 or 87-77-75-53-52-12.

With all the pieces placed, the position is as shown.

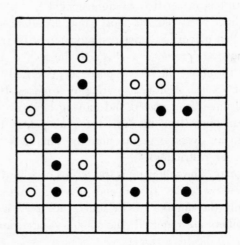

Move	White	Black
11	55-76	77-15T	Black threatens 87-47-65-75-53-33-15 or 87-47-56-53-33-15.
12	36-43	53-64T	Black threatens 87-47-46-64-24-15.
13	66-67T	62-34T	White threatens 41-43-76-67-23-28. Black threatens 83-47-46-64-34-33-15.
14	51-55	75-65T	Black threatens 85-65-64-34-33-15.
15	35-24	72-26T	Black threatens 85-65-47-46-26-15.
16	63-36	33-85T	Black threatens 85-65-64-34-45-15.
17	43-44	46-45T	Black threatens 85-65-47-45-34-16 or 85-65-47-45-34-52-12.

There is nothing White can do now. A move of 55-46T looks promising, but Black can answer with 64-63, completing a network of 85-65-63-52-34-45-15. White has lost.

TAKE IT AWAY is the name of the game and not, I hope, the verdict of the reader. Compared to FOCUS and NETWORK, which each demand extreme concentration to be played at the highest level, TAKE IT AWAY can, and should, be played in a relaxed manner.

TAKE IT AWAY is basically a development of the SOLITAIRE BOARD, expanding it from a solitary pastime to a competitive game for two or more players. The SOLITAIRE BOARD has been popular in Europe for several centuries and is now being sold in the United States under many different trade names.

There are two basic types of board, the English with 33 holes, and the French with 37 holes.

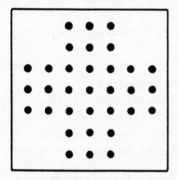 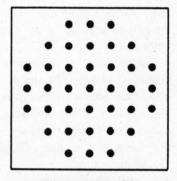

THE ENGLISH SOLITAIRE BOARD   THE FRENCH SOLITAIRE BOARD

The puzzle consists of filling all the holes except one, which is usually the center hole, with marbles and then, by a series of jumps, clearing off the marbles until only one remains. A jump is made orthogonally (which means that diagonal jumps are not allowed) over an adjacent marble into a vacant hole immediately on the other side.

TAKE IT AWAY
by Sid Sackson

● *Number of players.* Two, three, or four. When four play it can be each for himself, or in two teams. And with teams the partners can sit across from each other or next to each other, as the group prefers.

● *Equipment.* A checkerboard and 64 poker chips of three colors divided as follows: 34 white, 20 red, and 10 blue. The chips are placed on the board at random so that there is one on each space.

● *The play.* Choose the first player in any convenient manner. If a four-hand game is being played with the partners sitting next to each other, the first player should be chosen so that after his turn the opponents will have their turns. Play rotates to the left.

The first player removes any white chip (white being the least valuable) from the board and places it before him.

After this, all moves consist of a jump or a series of jumps. A jump is made in a straight line, either orthogonal or diagonal (which is allowable in TAKE IT AWAY), over an adjacent chip into an empty space next to the chip jumped. Any chip which is in position to do so, may be used for jumping. If, after the jump, the chip used is in position to make another jump (which may be in a different direction), the new jump must be made. And so on. At the end of his turn the player picks up all the chips that were jumped and places them before him.

● *Take It Away.* A player may decide to drop out at any time. At the beginning of a turn he simply announces "Take it away," and makes no further moves in the game. Play continues with the remaining players until all but one have announced "Take it away." This last player, known as the "patsy," continues jumping chips until no further jumps can be made. Chips remaining on the board are counted against the patsy.

● *Scoring.* Each player scores 3 points for each blue chip, 2 points for each red chip, and 1 point for each white chip. The chips remaining on the board are counted against the patsy at 3 times their regular value. The player (or team) with the highest score is the winner.

The players in advance may agree to set the penalty for chips remaining on the board at 2 times their regular value, or at 4 times their regular value. This choice, naturally, has a decisive effect on the timing of the game.

Variations:

1. The first eight plays of the game consist of taking a white chip from the board, after which the jumping moves begin. This makes for a real wide-open game.
2. Eliminate the dropping out. All players stay in the game until all possible jumps have been made and no player is penalized for chips remaining on the board.

This last variation, I have since discovered, is very similar to a game called LEAP-FROG, invented in 1898 by H. J. R. Murray, the author of *A History of Chess* and *A History of Board-Games Other than Chess.*

Five

GRAB
a
PENCIL

I F ALL THE PEOPLE who ever played TIC-TAC-TOE were laid end to end—they would promptly fall asleep. That's the kind of game it is. Yet put two people together with a pencil, a scrap of paper, and some time to kill and chances are they'll wind up playing endless games of T-T-T, with never a winner.

HOLD THAT LINE is a game I devised to fill just such an odd moment. It, too, is played with a pencil and a scrap of paper, but there is a challenge and a winner in each and every game.

HOLD THAT LINE   *by Sid Sackson*

A game for two players.

To play, just draw 16 dots in 4 rows of 4 (see illustration). The first player connects as many dots as he wishes in a straight line. From either end of the first line the second player draws another straight line. From either free end the first player now makes a line. Continue until no further lines can be drawn. The player who was forced to make the last line is the loser!

The completed line must be continuous, with no branches, no crossings, and no dot visited twice. The illustration shows a completed game which the second player has lost. The numbers on the lines are included to show the order in which they were played and, of course, do not have to be present in the actual game. Nor is it necessary to use different colors for the two players.

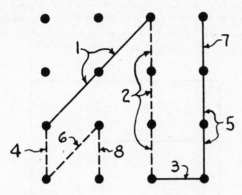

When you feel that you have mastered the game, try it with 25 dots placed 5 by 5, or with 24 dots placed 6 by 4.

CUTTING CORNERS is another escape from T-T-T. This one requires a little more equipment; a larger piece of paper and pencils of two colors, though in a pinch you can make do with one. It also requires a considerable amount of skill in determining just what corners to cut.

CUTTING CORNERS   *by Sid Sackson*

A game for two players.

On a piece of paper draw a good-sized square with one player's color on two adjacent sides and the second player's color on the other two.

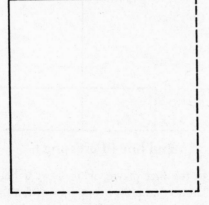

The starting square

The first player, starting at one edge, draws a line, makes one right-angle turn, and ends at another edge. At least one of the edges connected must be of the opponent's color.

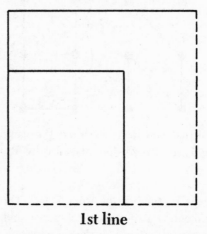

1st line

The second player now draws a similar line between two edges, making one crossing. This, as well as all subsequent lines, must either cross at least one line of the opposite color or must terminate in at least one edge of the opposite color.

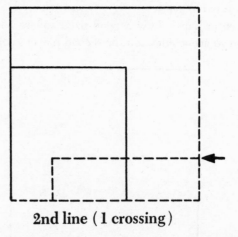

2nd line (1 crossing)

Play passes to the first player, who draws a line making exactly two crossings. The second player continues with a three-crossing line. The first player follows with a four-crossing line, and the second player finishes the game with a five-crossing line.

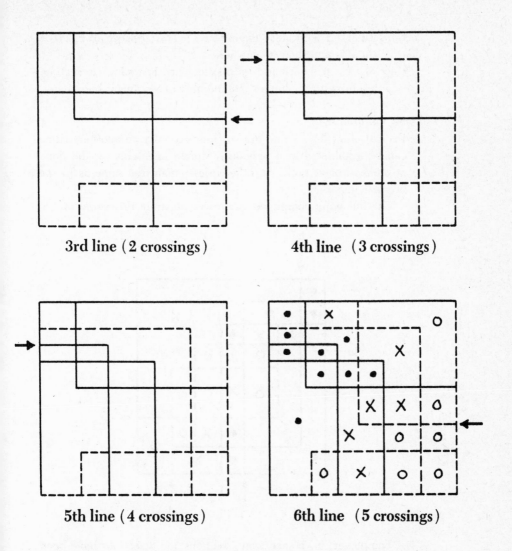

3rd line (2 crossings)

4th line (3 crossings)

5th line (4 crossings)

6th line (5 crossings)

The original square has now been divided into many sections (22 to be exact). A section is won by a player if he has more sides of his color around it than there are sides of the opponent's color. (For example, the lower left-hand section has 8 sides, 5 of which are the first player's color and 3 of which are the second player's. This section belongs to the first player.) If the sides are equally divided, it belongs to neither player.

The final diagram of the illustrative game shows the first player winning 9 sections, the second player winning 7 sections, and 6 sections (marked with an X) being tied. (This adds up to 22. If it doesn't, there is a mistake somewhere.)

A set of two games should be played, with first play alternating. The contestant with the higher total number of sections is the winner.

Some Variations:

1. Instead of all lines being drawn from one edge to another, a line can be terminated at a previously drawn line. This can be done at one end or at both. All other rules remain the same as in the original game.

    The following completed game will illustrate this variation.

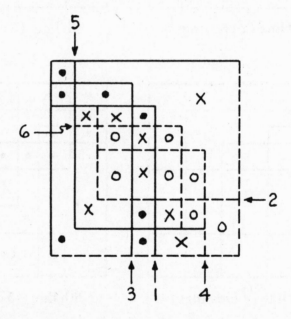

The players have each won 7 sections and 8 sections have been won by neither. (This again adds up to 22, which is also correct for this variation.)

2. The starting square can be varied by placing a player's color on opposite, instead of adjacent, sides. Or each player's color can be placed on only one side of the square, the other two sides being a neutral color which, when checking for control of a section, is not counted for either player.

3. Each player draws one more line, with 6 and 7 crossings respectively. With these extra lines the number of sections is raised to 37, so make sure you leave plenty of room.

STILL ANOTHER WAY of getting away from T-T-T is by trying some PAPER BOXING. This is essentially a double-board game, with each player constructing his own board. Then each player moves on this board, trying to outsmart the opponent. Although the setup is simple, the amount of strategic planning that can come into play is surprisingly great.

PAPER BOXING   *by Sid Sackson*

A game for two players. One is chosen, in any convenient manner, to be "even"; the other becomes "odd."

Each player takes a piece of paper and draws a grid of 4 by 4 squares, for a total of 16. Place the letter S, standing for "Start," in the upper left-hand square and then, each player hiding his choices, in the remaining 15 squares fill in the numbers from 1 to 15 in any desired pattern.

This accomplished, the papers are exposed and left in view for the duration of the game. Take the two numbers written in the lower right-hand square and add them together. If the result is even, the "even" player goes first; if odd, the "odd" player goes first.

The first player starts by moving to one of the squares next, including diagonally, to the Start square. He marks his move by drawing a line on his board from one square to the other. The second player then makes a similar move to a square of his choice on his board. The player who is in the square with the higher number has won the first round. With a tie, neither player gets the round.

The player winning the first round starts the second round. In case of a tie the same player who started the first starts the second. The move is made to any square adjacent to the last occupied square and, as before, the player in the higher numbered square wins the round.

Continue in this manner, with each move being made to a previously unused square, until all 15 have been used. The slugger who has won the greater number of rounds is the victor. If both win the same number, the victory goes to the one who played first at the start of the game (which is somewhat of a disadvantage).

If a player gets himself into a position where he cannot move because all adjacent squares have already been used, he loses by a "knockout" regardless of the number of rounds won. (This, of course, can only happen if he is careless.)

An illustrative game should help to clarify all of the above. The two players, whom we will call Even and Odd, filled in their boards as shown.

EVEN

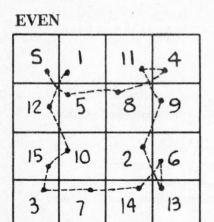

ODD

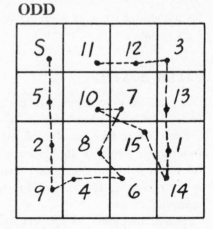

Adding the two numbers in the lower right-hand corner we find the total to be 27, so Odd plays first. In each round the numbers shown are the squares moved to by the two players; the underlined number indicates the player who moved first in that round.

Round	Even	Odd	
1	5	5̲	A tie.
2	8	2̲	Even leads: 1 to 0.
3	4	9̲	1 round each.
4	1̲1	4̲	Even ahead: 2 to 1.
5	9	6̲	Even again: 3 to 1.
6	2̲	8	Odd closing the gap: 3 to 2.
7	13	7	Even ahead: 4 to 2.
8	6	1̲0	Odd catching up: 4 to 3.
9	14	1̲5	Odd ties it up: 4 to 4.
10	7	1̲4	Odd pulls ahead 5 to 4.
11	3	1̲	Tied again: 5 to 5.
12	15	1̲3	Even on the offensive: 6 to 5.
13	1̲0	3	Even further in the lead: 7 to 5.
14	1̲2	12	A tied round.
15	1̲	11	Odd fights back, but too late.
			Final score: 7 to 6, favor of Even.

BATTLING WITH LETTERS to form abstruse words is without a doubt one of our most popular game forms. To most fans the advent of SCRABBLE marked the beginning of the era. However, there were many excellent word games before SCRABBLE.

As early as 1874, the F. A. Wright Company of Cincinnati published LOGOMACHY, OR WAR OF WORDS. This was played with 72 letter cards according to rules very similar to the game of CASINO. The player with the most cards at the end of the game scored 3 points for cards. Replacing the Aces were four prize cards—J, K, V, and X—worth 1 point each; and the Q and Z were double prizes worth 2 points each. A sweep, consisting of clearing all the cards from the table, scored 1 point. Twenty-one points were required to win. My collection contains a later edition of LOGOMACHY and the quaint, hand-tinted cards are a delight to play with.

LAST WORD was born one day when I was stranded with two word-game lovers far from any letter cards, letter dice, or letter tiles. Challenged, I devised a game using only an available pencil and some sheets of paper. I was rather surprised when it gained a considerable measure of popularity among my friends, some praising it as the "last word" in word games. The rules are very simple and yet it offers a wide scope in forming words, since players are free to choose their own letters.

LAST WORD   *by Sid Sackson*

A game for two, three, or four players.

On a sheet of paper draw a grid of 9 squares by 9 squares (for a total of 81 squares). In the 9 center squares fill in 9 letters taken at random from any piece of written material. As an example let us take the sentence "War of words is a game originally published in 1874" as a point of departure and make a setup as shown.

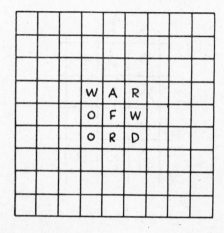

153

Choose for first, and play then rotates to the left.

Each player in turn places a letter in an empty space adjacent, including diagonally, to at least 2 letters already on the layout. Using this newly placed letter, and letters that are in line with it, words are formed. If desired, the letters from the layout can be rearranged in forming the word. For example, if the first player chooses to place the letter "D," as shown, he can form the word "Wood" in a vertical direction and the word "Wad" in a diagonal direction.

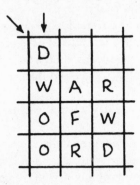

The player multiplies the length of each word formed and the result is his score. In the above example the score is 12 points (4×3). If a player can form more than one word in a direction, only the longest is counted. A player may not place a letter unless he can form words with it in at least two directions.

In forming a word in a particular line it is not necessary to use all of the letters in that line, but those used must be continuous with the letter placed. If the previous example is continued by the second player adding the letter "O," as shown, he can form the word "Do" horizontally, the word "Or" diagonally, and the word "Oaf" vertically. He could not use the "Oar" vertically since that would require skipping the "F."

The score for this play is 12 points ($2 \times 2 \times 3$).

To further illustrate the formation of words, let's extend the example by showing the next 9 letters to be placed, listing the words formed and the score for each play.

1. L—Flow (hor.), Low (up diag.), Lo (down diag.)= 24 points ($4 \times 3 \times 2$)
2. A—Ado (hor.), Ward (vert.) = 12 points (3×4)
3. N—Warn (hor.), Nor (diag.) = 12 points (4×3)
4. S—Wards (vert.), Owls (diag.) = 20 points (5×4)
5. M—Warm (hor.), Am (diag.) = 8 points (4×2)
6. T—Toad (hor.), Fort (diag.) = 16 points (4×4)
7. O—Woof (hor.), Tom (vert.), Or (diag.), Do (diag.) = 48 points ($4 \times 3 \times 2 \times 2$)
8. E—Rode (hor.), Tome (vert.), Wade (diag.) = 64 points ($4 \times 4 \times 4$)
9. T—Raft (vert.), Lot (diag.), Dot (diag.) = 36 points ($4 \times 3 \times 3$)

The game continues until a letter has been placed in at least one square along each of the four edges of the layout. As soon as the last edge has been reached the game is over and the player with the highest score is the winner.

• *Variation.* Once players are familiar with LAST WORD, they may prefer this variation, which brings about a greater variety in the letters chosen.

At the beginning of the game each player writes out a complete alphabet in a convenient area of the paper and every time he places a new letter on the layout he crosses it off his alphabet. A player can (and probably will) use some letters more than once, but he must try to use as many different letters as possible, since he is penalized for any unused letters remaining at the end of the game.

A player may place a letter which only forms a word in one direction. The score for this is as many points as there are letters in the word.

The game is ended when one player has used all of his letters. From their scores, the other players deduct 30 points each for an unused J, V, X, Q, or Z and 10 points each for any other unused letter.

For this variation a larger layout should be used: 11 × 11 for two players and 13 × 13 for three or four players.

THE GENESIS OF PATTERNS II is very clear. Bob Abbott, with his card game ELEUSIS (see the introduction to CROSSINGS in Chapter Two), opened up a whole new world to be explored, the world of inductive games. Martin Kruskal, of Princeton University, progressed further along the same path with another card game, DELPHI.

Martin Gardner, in his *Second Book of Mathematical Puzzles and Diversions*, struck out into new territory by introducing the idea of a game based on the intuitive guessing (hunches, in other words) of concealed visual patterns. Taking this proposal as a starting point, I developed PATTERNS II (II because PATTERNS, a card game in Chapter Three, was conceived earlier).

PATTERNS II allows, in fact requires, the player to formulate a hypothesis and then test it's validity by experimentation. If it stands up, it is probably right. If not, it must be changed to fit the new facts. And the player must be willing, if the experimental data fails to justify it, to throw out a hypothesis completely and come up with a new one. This process is, of course, what we call the scientific method.

PATTERNS II   *by Sid Sackson*

● *Number of players.* Three, four, five, or six.
● *The designer.* In each game one player is the "designer" who creates a pattern which the other players attempt to discover. It is

preferable to play in rounds so that all players have an equal number of chances at being the designer.

On a piece of paper the designer draws a 6 by 6 grid. He fills in the 36 squares of the grid using one or more of the following four symbols: ○, +, ∴, ☆. Although he is free to use any arrangement he wishes, it is to his advantage to set up a pattern that is strongly ordered, so that at least one of the other players will be able to discover it quickly. Actually the designer makes his best score when there is one guesser who does very well and another who does very poorly.

Here are some samples of patterns arranged, more or less, in order of difficulty, with the easiest first.

★	+	∴	★	+	∴
★	+	∴	★	+	∴
★	+	∴	★	+	∴
★	+	∴	★	+	∴
★	+	∴	★	+	∴
★	+	∴	★	+	∴

∴	∴	∴	○	○	○
∴	○	∴	○	∴	○
∴	∴	∴	○	○	○
○	○	○	∴	∴	∴
○	∴	○	∴	○	∴
○	○	○	∴	∴	∴

○	○	+	+	○	○
○	+	∴	∴	+	○
+	∴	★	★	∴	+
+	∴	★	★	∴	+
○	+	∴	∴	+	○
○	○	+	+	○	○

∴	+	○	○	+	∴
★	∴	+	+	∴	★
○	★	∴	∴	★	○
+	○	★	★	○	+
∴	+	○	○	+	∴
★	∴	+	+	∴	★

+	+	+	+	+	+
○	○	○	○	○	+
○	+	+	+	○	+
○	+	○	○	○	+
○	+	+	+	+	+
○	○	○	○	○	○

★	★	○	○	∴	∴
★	★	○	○	∴	∴
∴	∴	★	★	○	○
∴	∴	★	★	○	○
○	○	∴	∴	★	★
○	○	∴	∴	★	★

• *Determining the pattern.* While the designer is creating his pattern, each of the other players draws a 6 by 6 grid on a separate piece of paper which he identifies with his initials.

A guesser obtains information about the pattern by marking one or more squares on his grid with a slant line in the lower left-hand corner and passing the sheet, face down, to the designer. The designer fills in the proper symbols in all of the requested squares and passes the sheet, again face down, back to the guesser. There are no turns, and there is no limit either to the number of times a guesser may request information or to the number of squares requested each time.

When a guesser believes that he has determined the pattern, he fills in the remaining squares with symbols. To expedite the scoring, these guessed symbols are enclosed in parenthesis.

If a player feels that it is impossible for him to discern a pattern, he does not make any guesses. (He will receive a score of 0 but the designer will receive a penalty which, if a number of guessers give up, can be severe.)

● *Scoring.* When all the players have completed their guessing, or have given up, the master pattern is turned face up. Each player checks his guesses against the master pattern, scoring $+1$ for a correct guess and -1 for an incorrect guess. The result is the player's score and it is possible for a player, through wrong guesses, to end up losing points.

A player who did not make any guesses scores 0.

The designer scores twice the difference between the best score made by a guesser and the worst. If one player gives up without guessing, his score of 0, if it is the lowest, is used in determing the designer's basic score. However, 5 points are deducted from the designer's basic score as a penalty. For each additional player who gives up, the designer loses 10 more points from his basic score.

To show how the scoring works, let's take the results of several games played between four players—a designer (D) and three guessers $(A, B,$ and $C)$.

If A scores 18, B scores 15, and C scores 14, D's score is then 8 (which is twice the difference between 18 and 14).

If A scores 18, B scores 15, and C scores -2, D's score is then 40 (which is twice the difference between 18 and -2).

If A scores 12, B scores 7, and C scores 0 by giving up, D's score is then 19 (which is twice the difference between 12 and 0, with 5 points deducted).

If A scores 12, and B and C both score 0 by giving up, D's score is then 9 (which is twice the difference between 12 and 0, with 15 points deducted).

If A, B, and C all score 0 by giving up, D's score is then -25 (no basic score, since all guessers had the same score and 25 points deducted).

• *A sample of pattern guessing.* This is a sample, taken from an actual game illustrating some of the thinking I used in arriving at a pattern.

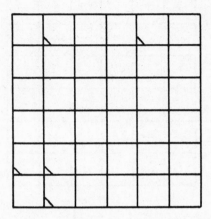

I mark the above 5 squares to see if I can discern any signs of symmetry. The grid comes back from the designer marked as shown (except for the four additional slant marks which are my next request).

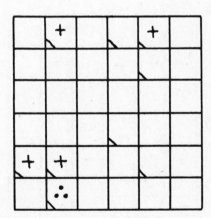

If I can find a + in the square below the + on the top line, there is a good chance that the pattern is symmetrical around the long diagonal running from top left to bottom right. And let's get some more information.

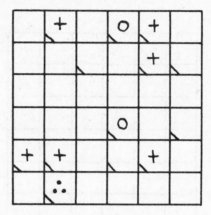

The + is just where I thought it would be. It looks as if there might be a line of +'s starting at the top and then turning and continuing to the left border. Let's check one more square. Also let's see if there is a line of ∴'s outside of the +'s by trying two squares in this line. Even if only the upper square contains a ∴, it will at least be further confirmation of the symmetry. The fourth slant is placed in a still unknown area.

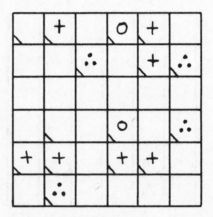

It is time to come up with a hypothesis. It looks as if there are no ☆'s, so let's say that the upper left-hand corner contains a ○. This is flanked by a line of +'s, followed by a line of ∴'s, a line of ○'s, another line of +'s, and another line of ∴'s on the outside. If the two requested squares don't show up with ○'s, there is something wrong with the hypothesis.

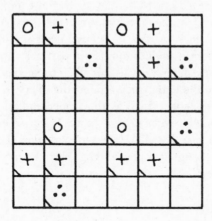

The ○'s show up as predicted, so I decide to take the plunge and fill out the rest of my grid as shown.

O	+	(∴)	O	+	(∴)
(+)	(+)	∴	(o)	+	∴
(∴)	(∴)	(∴)	(o)	(+)	(∴)
(o)	o	(o)	o	(+)	∴
+	+	(+)	+	+	(∴)
(∴)	∴	(∴)	(∴)	(∴)	(∴)

O	+	∴	O	+	∴
+	+	∴	O	+	∴
∴	∴	∴	O	+	∴
O	O	O	O	+	∴
+	+	+	+	+	∴
∴	∴	∴	∴	∴	☆

The pattern on the right is the original master pattern. Checking my guesses against it, I find that I have 20 correct and 1 wrong for a final score of 19 points.

The designer, incidentally, threw in the ☆ not to catch players who missed it but rather as a red herring in the path of those who did find it.

IN CHAPTER ONE I touched briefly on the history of THE LANDLORD'S GAME and how it blossomed into MONOPOLY. The former game, coming as it did at the beginning of this century, was the innovator of what has turned out to be one of the most important game ideas of the century, that of ownership of parts of the board by the players.

Some race games of an earlier period made use of the concept in a rudimentary form—the first to reach a particular space could exact a payment from a later arrival—but THE LANDLORD'S GAME was the first to fashion the entire play around the idea.

My game of PROPERTY is, as the name implies, also built around ownership and the collection of rents. It, however, has an entirely new approach, one that allows for a great deal of choice in the making of plays. And though it is played on a sheet of paper, it is really a full-fledged board game.

PROPERTY   *by Sid Sackson*

- *Number of players.* Two to six.
- *Equipment.* A good sized sheet of paper. Pencil and eraser. Standard deck of cards. Set of poker chips (50 white, 25 red, 25 blue).
- *The setup.* On the sheet of paper draw an 8 by 8 grid and mark the rows and columns as shown. If a red pencil is available it should be used for marking the columns, while a black pencil is used for the rows.

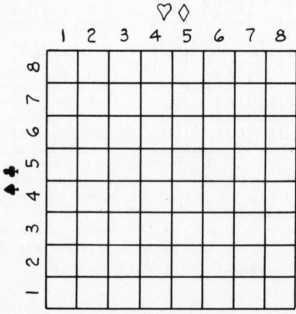

Remove all the pictures and the two Jokers from the deck of cards. These cards are given a "purchase" value as follows: King—4 units; Queen—2 units; Jack or Joker—1 unit. Divide the cards so that each player has the same number of units. When six are playing, each will get 5 units (for instance, a King and a Jack, or two Queens and a Joker). When five are playing, each will get 6 units. When four are playing, each will get 7 units. When three are playing, each will get 10 units. And when two are playing, each will get 14 units. (With four or two players the Jokers are not used.) These cards are placed face up on the table next to the players.

The poker chips are divided among the players in accordance with the following table. Chips left over are not used in the game.

No. of Players	White	Red	Blue
6	8	4	4
5	10	5	5
4	12	6	6
3	16	8	8
2	15	9	9

White chips are worth $1, red chips $5, and blue chips $10.

● *The hands.* The remainder of the deck (after removal of the pictures and Jokers) is shuffled and cut. High card (an Ace is considered as a 1) is first and play then rotates to the left.

The cards are reshuffled and placed face down on the table. From the top of the deck the first player draws two or more cards as his hand. If the first two cards drawn are of different colors, one red and one black, that completes his draw. If the first two cards are the same color, the player continues to draw until he draws one card of the opposite color. All the players draw a hand in a similar manner.

● *The play.* Each player in turn plays a red card and a black card from his hand. The two cards played designate a space on the grid in which, if it is empty, the player marks his initials, taking possession of the space. (For example, a player uses the ♡A and the ♣8 and places his initials in the upper left-hand space on the grid.)

A 9 or a 10 can be used to represent any number from 1 to 8, but does not change its color. (For example, a player uses the ♡A and the ♣10. He can place his initials in any space in the left-hand column. Another player uses the ◇9 and the ♣9 and can place his initials in any space he chooses.)

After completing his play the player draws one or more cards from the deck until his hand again consists of one card of one color and one or more cards of the other color. (For example, after making his play a player has three black cards in his hand. He draws cards from the deck until he picks up a red card.)

When the deck is exhausted, the previously played cards are shuffled and turned over as a new deck.

● *Paying rent.* A player who uses two cards that designate a space owned by an opponent must pay rent to that opponent.

The amount of rent is determined by counting the number of spaces the opponent owns in a connected group which includes the space played upon. (Spaces touching only at a corner are not considered as connected.) If a ♢ and a ♣ are used in designating the space, the rent is $1 (white chip) for each space. If, however, a ♠ or a ♡ is used in designating the space, the rent is doubled to $2 per space. And if both a ♠ and a ♡ are used, the rent is doubled twice to $4 per space.

In the situation illustrated, a player (other than J.B.) plays the ♢3 and the ♣5. He pays J.B. $6, since there are 6 spaces in the connected group. If he plays the ♡3 and the ♣5, or the ♢3 and the ♠5, the rent is $12. And if he plays the ♡3 and the ♠5, the rent is $24.

● *Purchasing property.* After a player has paid rent to an opponent he may, if he wishes, purchase the space upon which he paid the rent, provided he holds enough "purchase" units (these are the picture cards distributed at the start of the game) to give 1 unit for each space in the group. The purchase units are taken by the original owner of the property, who may use them for making future purchases of his own. The initials in the space are erased and replaced by those of the buyer.

In the above example the player paying rent on space 3-5 could purchase it by giving 6 units (such as a King, a Jack, and a Joker) to J.B. The suits used in the original play affect the amount of rent, but do not affect the number of purchase units required.

• *Playing on your own property.* When a player uses two cards that designate a space he himself owns, he is said to have "mortgaged" that piece of property. He places an asterisk in the corner of the space to indicate this. There is no compensation for mortgaging a piece of property and a player will do so only if forced to by his cards, or to avoid paying rent to an opponent.

When a player plays upon a piece of his own property that has already been mortgaged, he loses that piece of property. All the markings in the space are erased and it then can be occupied in the same manner as any other empty space.

If a player purchases a piece of property from another player which has a mortgage on it, the mortgage remains.

• *Ending the game.* When a player is required to pay a rent greater than his supply of money, he gives the owner of the property all of his money and is declared bankrupt.

As soon as one player is bankrupt the game is ended. Each player counts his money and the one with the largest amount is the winner, property not being considered.

For a longer game, particularly when five or six are playing, continue the game until two, or if desired, three, of the players are bankrupt. As soon as a player is bankrupt his property is vacated and can be reoccupied in the regular manner. This extended game should, of course, be agreed on before starting.

• *A few final remarks.* Often at the end of a game a player has a choice of spaces to play in, all of which will cause him to become bankrupt. To avoid hard feelings he should choose the space which will result in the lowest rent.

Some players prefer to count property as well as money in determining the winner. If this is agreed on in advance, each piece of property is counted as being worth $5. This applies only in counting a player's worth at the end of the game and property is never used in place of money in the payment of rents.

No trading and no deals other than those specifically mentioned in the rules should be allowed.

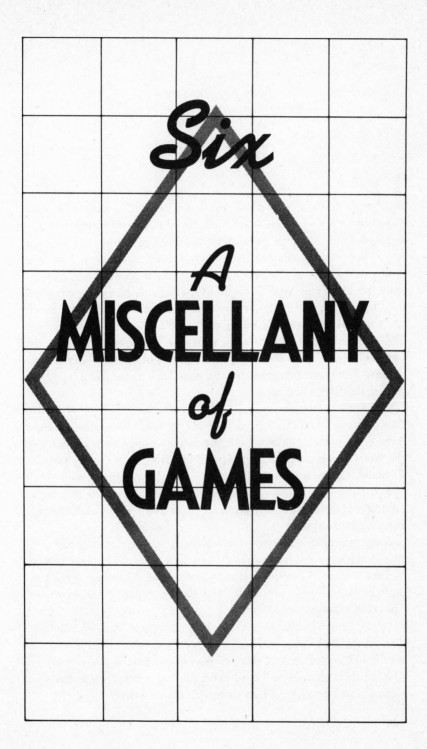

Six

A

MISCELLANY

of

GAMES

DICE are undoubtedly the oldest gaming device known to man. The ancient Greeks attributed their invention to Palamedes at the siege of Troy. Plutarch gave credit to the Egyptians; and bone or ivory dice, very similar to those now in use, have been found in tombs in the area of Thebes. The actual origin goes further back, to man's prehistory in Asia. Bones from the legs of sheep or goats were used by women and children for playing a game of skill, very much like the game of JACKS played by girls today. The bones were shaped like elongated dice and the men in the tribe began numbering the four rectangular sides and using them for gambling. At a later period, cubical dice were invented, but in Asia have never completely replaced the four sided dice.

The ancient Romans used both types of dice, calling the cubical dice "*tesserae*" and the four-sided variety "*tali*." The various throws were given names, the best being named for the goddess of love and the worst being called a dog. Gambling with dice was very popular in Rome, and rich men, in the later days of the empire, sometimes staked their fortunes on a single throw. The barbarians, too, were addicted to the craze and, having lost everything else, would gamble away their freedom.

Dice continued to be played so widely in Europe that in the Middle Ages there were academies in France where dice games were taught, and the makers of dice formed a separate guild. Dice were often prohibited, but never to any avail, and their popularity has continued unabated to the present time.

During World War II American prisoners of war in Germany flooded the Red Cross with requests for PARCHEESI sets. Finding the supply limited, officials of the Red Cross investigated and discovered piles of discarded game boards and playing pieces, while the dice were put to other uses. From then on, they sent dice.

With their long history, it is surprising how few games have been developed using dice, and most of these are purely gambling games offering little opportunity for exercising skill or making decisions. SOLITAIRE DICE is an attempt on my part to fill the gap. It is a game calling for considerable skill and a great deal of decision-making.

SOLITAIRE DICE   *by Sid Sackson*

● *Number of players.* One.
● *Equipment.* Five dice. A sheet of paper for marking the progress of the game.
● *The setup.* On the sheet of paper make a layout as shown. After they become familiar, it won't be necessary to include the values shown in parentheses.

```
(100)   2-
 (70)   3-
 (60)   4-
 (50)   5-          1-
 (40)   6-          2-
 (30)   7-          3-
 (40)   8-          4-
 (50)   9-          5-
 (60)  10-          6-
 (70)  11-
(100)  12-
```

● *The play.* The 5 dice are thrown and the player then divides the 5 numbers into two "combinations" of two dice each and one "reject." The two combinations are marked in the left column and the reject is marked in the one to the right.

(For example, the player throws a 1-1-2-4-5. One of the many ways in which this can be divided is by combining a 1 and the 2 to make a total of 3, combining the 4 and the 5 to make a total of 9, and leaving a 1 as the reject. The player places a mark next to the 3 and the 9 in the left-hand column and next to the 1 in the right-hand column.)

The player continues in this manner, throwing the 5 dice and dividing them as he chooses. He, however, is limited to 3 different reject numbers, and once marks have been placed next to 3 numbers in the reject column the player must divide the dice so as to have one of those 3 numbers as the reject.(For example, 1-2- and 5 have been

169

marked as the rejects. A throw is made of 1-4-4-4-6. The player has no choice but to divide the dice 4 & 4, 4 & 6, with 1 as the reject.)

If, after the reject numbers have been set, the player makes a throw containing none of these three numbers, he gets a "free ride." He can choose any two combinations he wishes and ignores the fifth die. (In the previous example, with 1-2- and 5 as the rejects, a throw of 3-4-4-6-6 would result in a free ride.)

The player may place marks next to as many numbers as he wishes in the combination column (and may sometimes be forced to use combinations against his will). If he marks too many different combinations, however, he is apt to be penalized in the scoring.

The player continues throwing the dice until one of the three reject numbers has 8 marks placed next to it. Play is then completed and the game is scored.

● *Scoring.* In order to score, a combination must have more than 5 marks next to it. For each mark over 5, the player receives the amount listed for that particular combination. (Thus if the player has 8 marks next to combination 6, he scores 120 points: 40 × 3.) A maximum of 5 marks over the initial 5 can be scored for any combination, even if more are placed next to it (because of the way the player decides to divide the throws of the dice). (Thus if the player has 11 marks next to combination 7, he scores only 150 points: 30 × 5.)

Each combination that has between 1 and 4 marks placed next to it causes a penalty of 200 points. A combination with 5 marks neither scores nor is penalized.

The following illustration of a completed game will show how the scoring works.

(100)	2-				
(70)	3- ~~HHt~~ 11	+140			
(60)	4- 1111		−200	1- ~~HHt~~ 111	
(50)	5-			2-	
(40)	6- ~~HHt~~ 111	+120		3- ~~HHt~~ 11	
(30)	7- ~~HHt~~ ~~HHt~~ 1	+150		4-	
(40)	8- 11		−200	5-	
(50)	9-			6- 1111	
(60)	10-				
(70)	11- ~~HHt~~ 111	+210			
(100)	12-				
		+620	−400		

170

The player's final score is $620 - 400 = 220$ points. (Incidentally, there are 40 marks in the combination column and only 19 in the reject column. This indicates that the player had one free ride.)

● *Winning the game.* The player naturally tries to make as high a score as possible, but if he reaches 500, he can consider himself a winner.

● *Competitive play.* Although intended for one player, SOLITAIRE DICE lends itself to competitive play by any number. Each player makes a layout for himself which he keeps hidden from the others.

One player is chosen to throw the dice and read out the results. Each player records the throws and plays them as he chooses. The dice are thrown until all of the players have finished (by having 8 marks placed next to a reject number). The layouts are then scored and the one who has made the most points is the winner.

ARTHUR AND WALD AMBERSTONE, the philosophic inventors of CUPS (see Chapter Two), were fascinated by Hermann Hesse's book *Magister Ludi* known in English as *The Bead Game.* In it, Hesse foresees the world guided through a period of threatened political upheaval by a monastic society of dedicated intellectuals. Their supreme achievement is "the bead game," an elaborate system of thought developed from the abacus and embracing all the arts and sciences.

Hesse never explains the workings of "the bead game" and the Amberstones decided to create their own. Using small chips of varied colors in place of beads, they experimented with the formation of intricate patterns. It was intriguing as a pastime, but never quite jelled as a game.

During a N.Y.G.A. meeting devoted to the bead game, Claude Soucie came up with the idea of using dominos in place of colored chips. This turned out to be the breakthrough I needed. By our next meeting I had developed the DOMINO BEAD GAME. Admittedly, it doesn't embrace all the arts and sciences, but it does call for some new thinking as you try to master a fascinatingly different set of relationships.

DOMINO BEAD GAME   *by Sid Sackson*

- *Number of players.* Two, three, or four.
- *Equipment.* Thirty dominos. Two sets of double-6 dominos are required. From each set remove all dominos containing a 6 or a blank, leaving 15 dominos in each set. (Dominos having a different color for each number are available and are particularly attractive for use in the DOMINO BEAD GAME.)
- *The setup.* From the face-down dominos each player draws one. High total will play first and play then rotates to the left.

All the dominos are reshuffled and each player draws the following number as his hand, which is kept hidden from the opponents:

> 14 dominos when two are playing
> 9 dominos when three are playing
> 7 dominos when four are playing

There are now 2 dominos remaining if there are two or four players, and 3 remaining if there are three players. In the latter case 1 domino is removed from the game, without being exposed, leaving 2 dominos. The last 2 dominos are placed with their long sides next to each other and then turned face up without altering their position. This is the "starter." (In the rare case that two identical doubles are turned as a starter, it is a misdeal and new hands and a new starter are drawn.)

- *Patterns.* In the play of the game dominos will be placed next to each other to form groups in a vertical and horizontal direction, similar to the way words are formed in a crossword puzzle. Each group must have a definite number pattern and a pattern is defined as soon as the same number appears twice.

Let's take a look at the example. In group A there are two 5s. The pattern is set as -5-5-5-. The pattern in group G is similarly set as -3-3-3-. Therefore space X can never be filled since it can't satisfy both patterns.

172

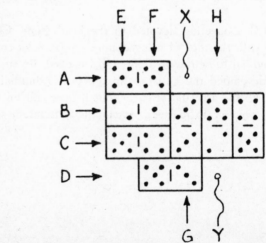

The pattern in group E is set as -5-2-5-2-. The pattern in group F is set as -5-1-4-5-1-4-. The pattern in group C is set as -5-4-3-2-5-4-3-2-. Although group B does not have a number appearing twice, the pattern is set because all five numbers are included. The next number of the right would have to be 2, while the next number of the left would have to be 4. The pattern in group B is therefore set as -2-1-3-5-4-2-1-3-5-4-.

In space Y a 2 could not be used because it would make group H incorrect. A 3 would similarly make group D incorrect. Any other number could be used in space Y.

● *The play.* Each player in turn places a domino so that *two* or more groups already on the table are correctly extended.

If 3 dominos have been placed in a row with their long sides in full contact, a fourth also in full contact on the long side cannot be added to either end.

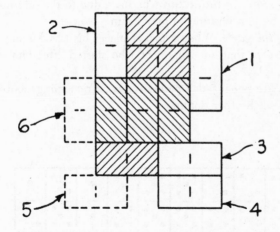

In the example 6 dominos, shown shaded, are already down. Domino #1 extends two horizontal groups. Domino #2 extends two horizontal groups and also a vertical group. Domino #3 extends a horizontal and a vertical group. Domino #4 extends two vertical groups. A domino cannot be placed in position #5 because only one group (vertical in this case) is extended. A domino cannot be placed in position #6 because that would place 4 dominos in a row with their long sides in full contact.

- *Scoring*. Each domino scores as it is placed and a running total is kept by the scorekeeper. The score is determined by counting the length of each extended group, including the newly placed domino, and multiplying the lengths. This score is doubled if the domino used is a double (such as 1-1, 2-2, etc.).

In the previous example domino #1 would score 12 points (3×4); domino #2 would score 60 points ($3 \times 4 \times 5$); domino #3 would score 20 points (4×5); and domino #4 would score 12 points (6×2). If any of the 4 dominos were a double, that particular score would be twice as great.

- *Inability to play*. If a player at his turn cannot find a position for any one of his dominos, he announces this and exposes his hand on the table. An opponent who sees an allowable play can, if he wishes, point it out and force the player to use it. If more than one play is pointed out, the player is free to choose the one he prefers.

If no play is pointed out, the player does not place a domino and makes no score. In future turns he may, due to the addition of new dominos, be in a position to play again.

- *Ending the game*. When a player places his last domino the game is over, except that any opponent who started after him is allowed one more play.

Players are penalized 5 points for each remaining double and 25 points for each other domino.

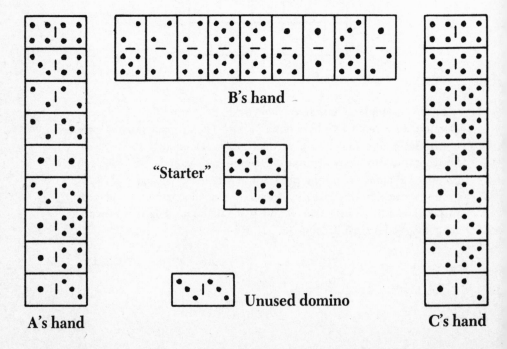

B's hand

"Starter"

Unused domino

A's hand

C's hand

The game is also ended if no player can place his remaining dominos. In this case all players lose points for their unused dominos.

The player with the highest resulting score is the winner.

* A *sample game*. The DOMINO BEAD GAME is not really difficult, but it is different! To gain a little familiarity with the play and the scoring let's take a look at a game played by three contestants, whom I will call A, B, and C.

The diagram at the left shows the hands, the "starter," and, since three are playing, the one unused domino.

A starts the play and at the end of the first round the layout looks as follows.

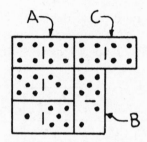

A scores 18 points ($3 \times 3 \times 2$—because of the double). B scores 9 points (3×3). And C scores 24 points ($4 \times 3 \times 2$—also because of the double).

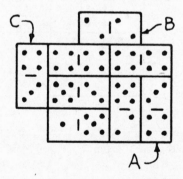

At the end of the second round the layout looks as above. A scores 48 points ($4 \times 4 \times 3$). B scores 32 points ($4 \times 4 \times 2$). And C scores 25 points (5×5). The totals are now: A—66, B—41, C—49.

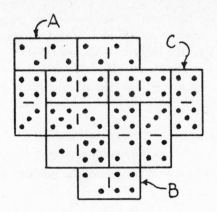

At the end of the third round the layout looks as above. A scores 96 points $(4 \times 3 \times 4 \times 2)$. B scores 25 points (5×5). And C scores 36 points (6×6). The totals are now: A—162, B—66, C—85.

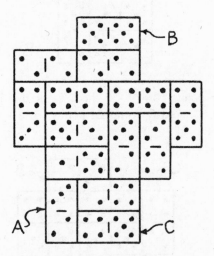

At the end of the fourth round the layout looks as above. A scores 18 points (6×3). B scores 72 points $(6 \times 6 \times 2)$. And C scores 147 points $(7 \times 7 \times 3)$. The totals are now: A—180, B—138, C—232.

At the end of the fifth round the layout looks as follows. A scores 32 points $(4 \times 4 \times 2)$. B scores 50 points $(5 \times 5 \times 2)$. And C scores 35 points (5×7). The totals are now: A—212, B—188, C—267.

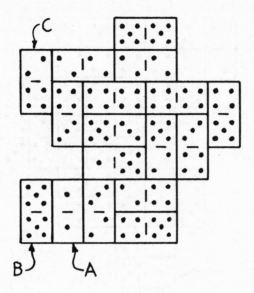

At the end of the sixth round the layout looks as below. A scores 24 points $(3 \times 4 \times 2)$. B scores 21 points (3×7). And C scores 20 points (5×4). The totals are now: A—236, B—209, C—287.

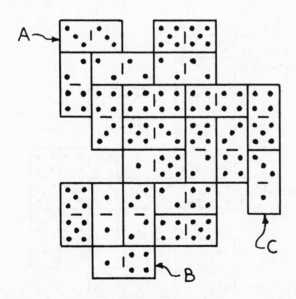

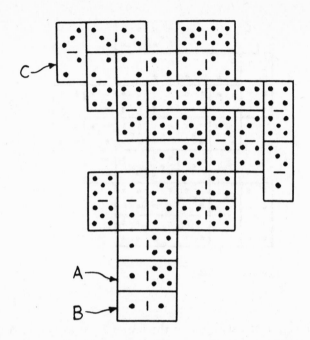

At the end of the seventh round the layout looks as above. A scores
32 points (4 × 8). B scores 90 points (5 × 9 × 2). And C scores
18 points (3 × 6). The totals are now: A—268, B—299, C—305.

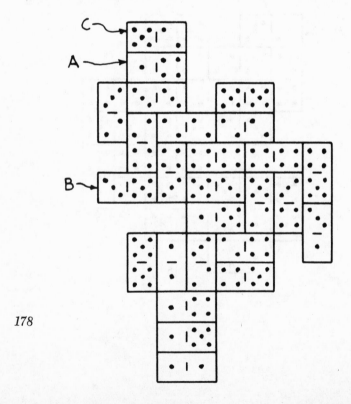

At the end of the eighth round the layout looks as bottom of preceding page. *A* scores 25 points (5 × 5). *B* scores 40 points (8 × 5). And *C* scores 36 points (6 × 6). The totals are now: *A*—293, *B*—339, *C*—341.

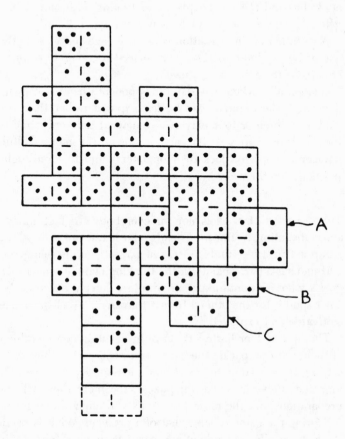

At the end of the ninth, and final, round the layout looks as above. *A* scores 12 points (6 × 2). The 1-3 could not be placed in the dotted position because, although the patterns match, it would result in four dominos being lined up with their long sides in full contact. *B* scores 35 points (7 × 5). And *C* scores 16 points (8 × 2). Since all the dominos have been placed, there are no deductions for unplayed dominos. The final score is *A*—305, *B*—374, *C*—357; and *B* is the winner.

• *A few words for advanced players.* Arthur and Wald propose a two-hand variation that eliminates the luck of the draw. Each player takes one set of 15 dominos so that each begins with the same hand. There is no starter, the first player simply starting with any domino he wishes and the second player continuing with one of his choice. After this, the game proceeds as in the regular game.

A variation on the variation is to have each player secretly choose one of his 15 dominos. These are placed together to form a starter. Otherwise the game is as above.

Incidentally, when two play the opponent's hand is known, so that if desired, the dominos can be left exposed rather than concealed. And with three or four players a somewhat different game results if the hands are exposed. The play is slower, but more skillful, as the players attempt to block their opponents and to force high scoring positions for themselves.

THE GAME OF HAGGLE is not for everybody. In fact I had doubts about including it. But my friends who like it are a most vociferous group and insisted, under threat of boycott, on its being presented.

HAGGLE is a party game for the thinking man, or woman. However guests who are nonthinkers, or who just don't want to be bothered, don't spoil it for the others. In fact they make excellent patsies to be cultivated and exploited.

The host and/or hostess do have to devote a considerable amount of thought to preparing the game. In essence, what they are doing is setting up an elaborate puzzle for their guests to solve. The more ingenious they can make the puzzle, the more they will enjoy the preparations and the more the guests will enjoy playing.

Scoring the game is somewhat of a problem. What is needed, and they are usually available at any party, is three or four "brains" who enjoy wrestling (and occasionally throwing verbal punches at each other) with problems in logic. When the game is completed the rest of the group can forget about the whole thing until the scorers finish their deliberations. Then the winners are announced and the prizes distributed.

(For those who are still not convinced I'll throw in, at no additional cost, the NO GAME which is simple to play and requires practically no preparation. Just skip HAGGLE and proceed directly to No.)

HAGGLE   *by Sid Sackson*

The setup for HAGGLE varies with the number of players, with the preferences of those preparing the game, and also with the necessity of making changes if part, or all, of a group has played before. The following actual game, one that involved fifteen participants, illustrates the equipment required and the general rules of play. You can take it from there.

● *Equipment.* Small blank cards in five different colors. 3″ × 5″ index cards cut in half make an ideal size. They can be obtained in yellow, blue, red, orange and, of course, white. (Green is also obtainable, but it is not a good idea to use both blue and green since they can be confused.) You will need twice as many of each color as there are players in the game. (Thus for fifteen players, thirty cards of each color were prepared.)

Secret information sheets. These are slips of paper on which information concerning the values attached to the colored cards are typed or printed. One piece of information is required for each player in the game and two slips are prepared for each piece of information. (Thus for fifteen players, thirty information sheets were prepared.)

The following are the information sheets used in the actual game:

1. Orange cards have a basic value of 4 and are equal to a red card and a yellow card.
2. White cards have the highest basic value and are equal to a red card and a blue card.
3. Blue cards have a basic value twice that of yellow and half that of orange.
4. If a player has more than three white cards, all of his white cards lose their value.
5. A player can score only as many orange cards as he has blue cards.
6. If a player has five or more blue cards, 10 points are deducted from every other player's score.
7. A set of three red cards protects you from one set of five blue cards.
8. The player with the most yellow cards gets a bonus of the number of cards squared. (For example, if most yellow cards are 5, bonus is 25.) If two or more players tie for most yellow, they are eliminated and bonus goes to the next highest.

9. If a player hands in seven or more cards of the same color, he is eliminated from the game.
10. Each set of five different colors gives a bonus of 10 points.
11. If a "pyramid" is handed in with no other cards, the value of the hand is doubled. A pyramid consists of four cards of one color, three cards of a second color, two cards of a third color, and one card of a fourth color.
12. The player with the most red cards doubles their value. In case of a tie, no player collects the extra value.
13. Each set of two yellow cards doubles the value of one white card.
14. Each set of three blue cards quadruples the value of one orange card.
15. No more than thirteen cards in a hand can be scored. If more are handed in, the excess will be removed at random.

● *Preliminary.* All of the cards are well shuffled and then dealt into piles of ten cards each. Each pile of cards is placed in an envelope together with two information sheets (chosen at random, except that duplicates should not be placed in the same envelope).

● *The play.* As early as possible in the evening the envelopes are distributed, one to each guest, with the following explanation.

The object of the game is to collect the most valuable hand of cards. In order to learn what constitutes a valuable hand you will have to read as many of the information sheets as possible. As you begin to obtain information you will want to get hold of certain cards and, possibly, to get rid of others. You are free to approach any other player at any time with a proposition to trade information or cards, or both. And, of course, it pays to haggle over the terms in an attempt to gain the most and give up the least.

At an appointed time (midnight is usually a good choice) you will place your cards in an envelope, mark it with your name, and hand it in for scoring. If you feel it is to your advantage, it is permissible to omit some of the cards you hold at the end of the game from those submitted as your hand.

● *Scoring the hands.* Each hand is scored taking into consideration all the data supplied on the information sheets.

Using the fifteen pieces of information from the game we have been following, let's take a look at the scoring of some of the hands. The basic values of the colors (which can be deduced from the first three information sheets) are: yellow $= 1$, blue $= 2$, red $= 3$, orange $= 4$, and white $= 5$.

Hand #1 consists of B-B-B-B-B-B-R-O-O-O-W. The six blue cards score 12 points. The red card scores 3 points. Two orange cards score 16 points each (see information sheet 14) and the third scores 4 points. The white card scores 5 points. The total score is 56 *points*. The blue cards also cause every other player to lose 10 points (see information sheet 6).

Hand #2 consists of Y-Y-Y-B-B-R-R-O-O-O-W-W-W, thirteen cards, which is the maximum that can be scored (see information sheet 15). The three yellow cards score 3 points. The two blue cards score 4 points. The two red cards score 6 points. Only two of the three orange cards can be scored (see information sheet 5) at 4 points each for a total of 8 points. One white card scores 10 points (see information sheet 13) while the other two score 5 points each for a total of 20 points. There are 20 points in bonuses (see information sheet 10) but there is also a deduction of 10 points for player #1's five blue cards. The final score is *51 points*.

Hand #3 consists of B-B-R-R-R-R-R-O-O-W-W. The two blue cards score 4 points. The five red cards are the largest number of this color in any hand and double their value (see information sheet 12) to a total of 30 points. The red cards also protect against the deduction for five blue cards (see information sheet 7). The two orange cards score 8. The two white cards score 10. The total score is *52 points*.

Hand # 4 consists of Y-Y-Y-Y-B-B-R-R-R-W. The four yellow cards score 4 points. The two blue cards score 4 points. The three red cards score 9 points, and protect against a deduction. The one white card scores 10 points (see information sheet 13). This totals to 27 points and since the hand is a pyramid (see information sheet 11) this doubles to *54 points*, the final score.

Hand #5 consists of Y-Y-Y-Y-Y-Y-R-W-W. The six yellow cards (one more would have voided the hand—see information sheet 9) score 6 points. The one red card scores 3 points. The two white cards score 20 points. The six yellow cards are the largest number of this color and earn a bonus of 36 points (see information sheet 8). This adds up to 65 points, but there is a 10-point deduction for the five blue cards, so the final score is *55 points*.

● *A few final remarks.* For obvious reasons the host and/or hostess cannot participate actively in the game. They should be available for answering questions and, particularly at the start of a game, there are bound to be plenty of these.

The first thing a player has to do in order to play well is to gain information as quickly as possible. Deals for exchange of information can take many forms. Players can agree to trade sheets, sight unseen, but run the risk of getting information they already have. Or players can tell each other the sheet number before trading. The deal can involve reading another player's sheet without actually gaining possession of it or even being told about the contents of a sheet without seeing it. In the latter case it is possible to obtain misinformation either by accident or by design.

A player should keep track of the sheet numbers he has seen and, unless he has a good memory, it is desirable to make notes about their contents. It is not always possible to obtain all the information nor is it always necessary. A player with a little information and a lot of luck can collect a hand of cards that just happen to fit together well enough to win.

A clever, but dirty, trick is for a player to obtain possession, early in the game, of two information sheets with the same number. He can then drive a hard bargain from those who want to see this information or can simply refuse to let anyone see it.

A player can ask for a card or cards as part of a deal in exchanging information. He can also stipulate, providing of course that the other player agrees, that he can choose the card or cards at a later time.

The above is not meant to cover all the possible forms that trading can take since any deal that two, or more, players agree on can be made. The ultimate, to my knowledge, in hard dealing occurred in one game when a player insisted upon, and received, the prize as payment for helping the other player win it.

As promised, here is the No Game. This is not one that I created myself, though I wish I had. It is a great party game, taking fifteen minutes to prepare, one minute to explain, and as much time to play as the guests wish to devote to it.

THE NO GAME   *Anon.*

You will need some red ribbon, cut into pieces about an inch long, one for each guest. Mount each piece on an ordinary straight pin and as the guests arrive decorate them with a ribbon.

When the assemblage is complete give them the following speech.

"You are competing to collect the most ribbons, and the way to get ribbons away from an opponent is get him to say 'No' to you. As soon as he utters the forbidden word you can cheerfully swipe all of his ribbons, even if he has a whole chestful.

"Any other form of negation, such as 'Absolutely not!' 'Drop dead!' or a slap in the face, is perfectly permissible, but once you say 'No,' good-bye ribbons.

"At the stroke of ——— (fill in as desired) the sneakiest player, who has collected the most ribbons, will be declared the winner and will be suitably rewarded with a lavish prize."

I HAVE ALWAYS been an inverterate fiddler. In one of my earlier jobs, my superior, after a number of nerve-wracking sessions, would not permit me to approach his desk before transferring every remotely movable object well out of my reach.

But every bad habit has its compensations. One day, with nothing else available to satisfy my craving, I pulled a handful of coins from my pocket and began to push them around on a convenient flat surface. Before long the random shifting had become systematized and the solitaire game of CHANGE CHANGE had been born.

CHANGE CHANGE   *by Sid Sackson*

● *Number of players.* One.
● *Equipment.* Eleven coins—four of one denomination, four of a second denomination, two of a third denomination, and one of a fourth denomination. (For example—4 pennies, 4 dimes, 2 nickels, and 1 quarter.)
● *The play.* Shake the eleven coins together in your hand and then place them on a flat surface arranged in three rows as shown. (The X represents an empty space.)

O   O   O   O
O   O   O   O
O   O   O   X

The object is to rearrange the coins into a symmetrical position by sliding them one at a time into the empty space (which, of course, is constantly changing its position). Only a coin directly next to the space, not including diagonally, can be moved into it.

A symmetrical position is one which is balanced around the middle row. In other words, if there is a penny in the top row, there must be a penny directly below it in the bottom row, etc. The single coin and the empty space, since there is only one of each, must always end up in the middle row.

● *A sample game.* In recording a game the spaces are lettered as follows.

A	B	C	D
E	F	G	H
I	J	K	L

Since there is only one place a moved coin can go, all that is required is to record the starting space.

Let's take a game played with the eleven coins previously mentioned. After mixing them they are put down like this.

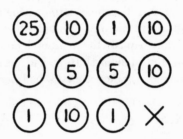

The moves are

1. H	9. F	17. K	25. H	33. I	41. F
2. D	10. E	18. G	26. L	34. J	42. B
3. C	11. I	19. C	27. K	35. F	43. A
4. B	12. J	20. D	28. G	36. B	44. E
5. F	13. K	21. H	29. F	37. A	45. I
6. E	14. G	22. L	30. B	38. E	46. J
7. A	15. F	23. K	31. A	39. I	47. K
8. B	16. J	24. G	32. E	40. J	48. G

and the symmetrical position is

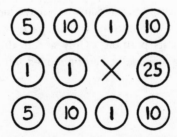

Another, and better, way of playing from the same starting position would be

1. K	5. I	9. C	13. A	17. K	21. F
2. J	6. J	10. B	14. B	18. L	22. B
3. F	7. F	11. F	15. C	19. H	23. C
4. E	8. G	12. E	16. G	20. G	24. G

leading to the symmetrical position

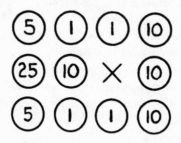

• *Winning.* Play seven games, keeping track of the number of moves required to reach symmetrical positions. If the seven can be completed in 100 or less moves, it is a win.

As you busily push pennies, nickels, dimes, and quarters around I will take leave. If you have had half as much pleasure from reading about and playing these games as I had from collecting, coaxing (from my fellow inventors), and creating them, I am very gratified.

Short Reviews of Games in Print

THE INFORMATION in this section is presented to help guide the reader who is interested in purchasing a game or an entire library of games. I have limited myself to games that are intended for an adult audience, and also those that can be played by the entire family without putting the parents to sleep.

But there has been such an explosion of adult level games in recent years that I have been forced to omit certain types of games in order to keep this section within manageable bounds. These are:

1. Electronic games—which constitute a world of their own.
2. War and fantasy games that take hours to learn and days to play. A sampling of simpler ones is included.
3. Sports games with detailed information appealing primarily to fans of that sport. Again some simpler ones are included.
4. Quiz games, or other games depending on specific knowledge that is quickly mastered.
5. Purely physical games.
6. Puzzles, even though they may be called games.
7. Standard games, such as Bingo, which are published by many firms.

You will notice that I haven't given ratings to the games. I prefer games that depend on skill rather than luck, but that is my personal preference and I would hesitate to inflict it on others. I attempt instead to give some idea of what the game is about, the mechanics of play, and the proportion of luck and skill involved.

The games are divided into a number of different categories and are listed alphabetically within each. There will probably be some objections to the way in which I have made the division but games, being a varied group, don't fit neatly into pigeonholes. Following each game is the name of the manufacturer; in a few cases the name of a principal distributor of the game is included following a slash.

I have attempted to make this information as up-to-date as possible but new games do come on the market and, unfortunately, some games die. Locating a particular game can sometimes present a problem. Checking a number of stores, including those calling themselves "hobby shops," will frequently do the job. If all else fails I can supply the manufacturer's address. But, please, include a self-addressed envelope.

If you find any goofs I would greatly appreciate hearing about them. And if I have missed a game that should have been included, I would love to hear about it for the next edition.

*For British manufacturers, see page 221

FINANCIAL GAMES—*where making money is the object.*

ACQUIRE by Sid Sackson (Avalon Hill). By placing tiles on a board, hotel chains are built, invested in, and merged. Rules are simple but the opportunity for strategic planning and control of the outcome is great. Two to 6 players.

ANTI-MONOPOLY (National Games). Sets of three spaces each represent a monopoly to be broken. Landing allows a player to purchase an "indictment" marker. Markers on two spaces assign that case to a player, who gains money and "social credit" for finishing the job. Two to 6 players.

ANTI-MONOPOLY II (National Games). Players choose to be a "competitor" or a "monopolist." A competitor can build houses on a property even if only one of a group is owned. A monopolist must own two in a group in order to build, but gets higher rents for fewer houses. Two to 6 players.

BUSINESS STRATEGY (Avalon Hill). As the heads of giant corporations, players bid for raw materials, erect factories, manufacture products, offer them for sale in a limited market, and try to avoid bankruptcy. Advanced rules bring in many more business decisions. Two to 4 players.

CALIFORNIA GOLD RUSH GAME, THE (Arrowhead Gold Rush Company). Mainly a matter of buying gold mines and other properties, developing them, and collecting when others land. "Lady Luck" cards also pack a punch. The exotic locale is well developed. Two to 6 players.

CARTEL—THE INTERNATIONAL OIL GAME (CGS/Art Fair). A world map shows five oil fields in each of six continents. Bidding spaces in the surrounding path call for a field to be auctioned. When all fields in a continent are owned, a vote of four of the five owners can form a cartel, upping the oil's price. Two to 6 players.

COMMODITY HOUSE (EHP). A player landing on a space for one of three commodities causes a unit to be sold in a novel auction. The value of the units goes up as certain cards are faced, but players usually can't wait for a top price. Two to 4 players.

EASY MONEY (Milton Bradley). Played with dice on a board having "property" spaces on the four edges. When landed on, these are auctioned to the highest bidder. After buying a space on each edge a player can build houses on any of his spaces and increase his rental. Two to 6 players.

ECONOMY GAME, THE (Cadaco). A simple but clever "market" using chips placed on spaces from $100 to $500 involves the players in the problems of supply and demand. Many more business options are included. Two to 6 players.

FORTUNE 500 (Pressman). Players attempt to triple their capital by investing wisely, producing and selling products profitably, and taking advantage of the services of banks, insurance companies, and advertising agencies. Three to 8 players.

GOLD (Avalon Hill). Charts give indications of how investments will be affected by board spaces, cards, and die

189

throws. As they move up or down, owners collect or pay for the change at once. Considerable opportunity to influence opponents' fortunes. Two to 8 players.

IN THE CHIPS (Tega). As players pass through Silicon Valley (other locations available) they are constantly making financial decisions. They can invest in education, real estate, cars, or various enterprises. The pros and cons of each are nicely balanced. Two to 6 players.

MARKET MADNESS (Yaquinto). Buy and sell shares in five commodities, using information from "fluctuation" cards and actions of previous players. Optional rules move prices by purchases and sales, and allow buying on margin and selling short. Two to 8 players.

*MONOPOLY (Parker Brothers). The first "property" game to catch on and still going strong. Moves determined by dice but the necessity of obtaining a "monopoly" in order to build houses calls for considerable trading skill. Two to 10 players.

NET WORTH II (Retire Facts). Investments are made in savings, oil, cattle, real estate, or stocks of three different performance levels. Players buy, sell, and collect only on their own side of the board. A special backward move can be very lucrative. Two to 4 players.

RICH FARMER/POOR FARMER (McJay Game Company). Players can buy farms by landing on the proper spaces. Farms are developed by plowing, fertilizing, planting, and gathering, each step increasing the charge to an opponent landing. Two to 6 players.

STOCK MARKET (Whitman). Speculate in six different stocks by moving, by dice throw, along a path and buying stock in the company landed upon. Sell when the price is right or when forced to. Dividends and stock splits, too. Two to 6 players.

STOCK MARKET GAME, THE (Avalon Hill). Invest in five types of securities, from blue chip to speculative. Players place markers on the "trading post" to indicate buys or sells. Prices change depending on the spread, and a faced market trend card. One or more players.

STOCKS & BONDS (Avalon Hill). A realistic stock market game. Players invest in a choice of ten securities with varying potential, risk, and yield. Prices change through chance, but tend to average the listed performance. Two to 8 players.

TYCOON (Wattson Games). As players move around the board buying and selling stock, the prices change with each dice throw. Spaces landed on can bring rewards or penalties, and sometimes opportunities to negotiate a deal or to blackmail an opponent. Two to 6 players.

WORLD GAME OF ECONOMICS (John N. Hansen). Appropriately packaged in a handsome carrying case. Although neatly tied to economic factors, the game is basically a question of moving markers, by a combination of luck and skill, to land in scoring spaces. One to 6 players.

WORLD WEALTH (EHP). Landing in the proper spaces allows purchase of raw materials, conversion to finished goods, and foreign sales. Investment in machinery allows a player to throw a die and purchase, or convert, that many units for the price of one. Two to 4 players.

WAR AND BATTLE GAMES—*which imitate one of man's oldest pursuits. Chess, at its start, was based on war as fought at that time.*

ACE OF ACES (Nova Game Designs). A very novel game of air combat in World War I. Each player uses a book with 223 pictures showing views from a cockpit. As players maneuver they are directed to new pages, clevely coordinated to keep the proper relationships. Two to 12 players.

AFRIKA KORPS (Avalon Hill). The Desert Fox, Rommel, *vs.* the allies in North Africa. Good for beginners since it is one of the simplest of the A.H. battle games.

AXIS AND ALLIES (Nova Game Designs). World War II fought on a map of the world divided into land and sea areas. Army, navy, air, and industrial units are coded by shape and size for easy identification. A simple die throw for each unit in a battle determines whether it hits or not. Five down to 2 players.

BARBARIANS, THE (Yaquinto). Two separate games are included. In "Sack Rome" two or three players take turns seeing how long it takes to capture Rome. In "Mongol" two play and the Mongol attempts to occupy the civilized world in a set time.

BATTLE (Yaquinto). This is an excellent introduction to war gaming. In the basic game each player has only ten combat units and the rules are quite simple. Optional rules increase the complexity. Movable terrain can alter the field. Two players.

BLUE & GRAY (SPI). Another good introduction to war gaming, where cardboard counters move on hexagon battlefields. Four pages cover the standard rules, with separate additions and playing material for each of four Civil War battles. Two players.

BLUE & GRAY II (SPI). Four more Civil War battles using the same standard rules. Two players.

COMMAND SHIP INVASION (McJay Game Company). Players move ships of three types by the throw of three dice. One indicates the type that can move, one gives the distance, and one sets the color of the landing space—or the chance of a remote hit on an enemy ship. Two players.

CONQUEST (Conquest Games). Using molded pieces representing soldiers, elephants, chariots, knights, and ships, war is conducted along intermeshed paths on land and sea. Several pieces can be moved on a turn, up to a total movement of twenty spaces. Separate editions for 2 or for 4 players.

*DIPLOMACY (Avalon Hill). Fought on a map of pre-World War I Europe. Before each simultaneous move, players confer for fifteen minutes making deals, with possible double-cross in mind. Best for 7 players, but as few as 3 can play.

FALL OF SOUTH VIETNAM, THE (Yaquinto). Played on a map of South Vietnam divided into twenty provinces, and showing incursion routes from Cambodia. Frequent die throws for troops and for combat resolution. The North wins by occupying Saigon in eight turns. Two players.

FEUDAL (Avalon Hill). A cross between Chess and a war game. The various pieces, including castles, peg into a plastic board and the starting positions are set up in secret. All pieces can be moved during a turn. Two, 4, or 6 players.

FINAL FRONTIER (Ral Partha). Quite similar in set up and play to Galactic Grenadiers.

FIRE WHEN READY (Metagaming). Using counters representing battleships, cruisers, destroyers, and torpedo boats, various sea battles can be fought. It takes concentration to master the rules, and a bit of paper work to handle the records. One or more players.

4000 A.D. (Waddingtons). Space is divided into sectors on two levels, stars on the lower level being smaller and dimmer. Ships travel, for exploration and battle, by "space warps." These leave a sector, move along a track each turn, and reappear in a sector that many "spaces" away in any direction. Two to 4 players.

GALACTIC GRENADIERS (Ral Partha). Played on a four foot by four foot flat area, using cardboard pieces to set up a terrain. Forty quite small metal figures do the fighting. Movement and firing of weapons is measured in inches. Two players.

G.E.V. (Steve Jackson Games). War as fought in the 21st century. Although relatively "small" in the number of unit counters supplied, the rules are quite complex, covering all aspects of war gaming. One or 2 players.

HOUSE DIVIDED, A (GDW). The broad sweep of the American Civil War. Simpler than most war games (for instance, instead of all pieces moving, a die throw sets the number of "marches") but all aspects are covered. An excellent introduction. Two players.

IMPERIALISM (Flying Buffalo). Travel across the sea to establish colonies. Die throws indicate the wealth potential, which can be used for armies and fleets; or for ports, cities, and fortifications, which are marked by grease pencil on the plastic surface. Two to 8 players.

OGRE (Steve Jackson Games). An "ogre" is a supertank of future wars. In the basic scenario one player uses a strength allotment to set up a defense against a single ogre. Advanced scenarios add to the forces in the battle. Two or 3 players.

ONE-PAGE BULGE (Steve Jackson Games). The famed "Battle of the Bulge" in World War II. This is a full war game with concise, but complete, rules. A good way of familiarizing beginners with the genre. Two players.

RAID ON IRAN (Steve Jackson Games). The U.S. attempt to rescue the hostages from the embassy. Surprise is introduced by the use of face down counters, including dummies, and special advantages chosen by each side. Two players.

*RISK (Parker Brothers). Players skillfully deploy their armies on a map of the world and then try to invade their neighbors, using dice in an interesting manner for resolving battles. New armies are raised from the controlled territories. Win by conquering the world. Two to 6 players.

SEASTRIKE (Ariel/Fantasy Games Unlimited). Players secretly choose a naval force, within a fixed budget. These are maneuvered on an ocean area formed by four boards. One indicator measures each ship type's movement and another handles the firing range. Two players.

SOLDIER KING (GDW). This is a simplified—but quite rich in detail—game of battle and diplomacy. Each player attempts to expand his kingdom and, by occupying four of the seven "crown" cities, become emperor. Four players.

STARFIRE (Task Force). A tactical battle in space with as few as one ship per player. The ships' offensive and defensive characteristics are noted by letters on a sheet of paper, which are crossed off as the ship is damaged. Two or 3 players.

STARFIRE II (Task Force). More tactical battles in space, with the addition of a fast one-man fighter. Two or 3 players.

STRATEGO (Milton Bradley). Each player has forty pieces whose identity only he can see. The Marshal is the strongest piece and only a Spy can capture him. Scouts are useful for probing. Bombs are used for defense, particularly of the Flag. Two players.

SUPERIORITY (Yaquinto). Playing on two identical fields screened from each other, each player tries to move his forces forward. Missiles are launched in an attempt to eliminate enemy units. Units have varying "victory points." Two players.

TACTICS II (Avalon Hill). The original A.H. battle game. A comparatively simple abstract campaign where players maneuver infantry, armored, paratroop, and amphibious divisions. Two players or teams.

WARPWAR (Metagaming). Players design their space ships using an allotted number of "build points," and can use points for repairing damaged ships. In combat, each ship can secretly choose a tactic, a target, and how its strength is allocated. Two players.

FANTASY GAMES—*where battles, expeditions, and other adventures involve monsters, mythology, and/or magic.*

AMOEBA WARS (Avalon Hill). Interstellar warfare against enemy lords, doomsday machines, and space amoebas. Numbered "power cards" allow each player of a higher card to use all those below. Win by occupying the central star. Two to 6 players.

ATTACK OF THE MUTANTS (Yaquinto). The "human" player sets up walls in the science building to try to prevent the "mutants" from reaching the "tech room" in the center of the building. Mutants smash their way through doors. Combat involves all units in the same room. Two players.

CAVERNS DEEP (Ral Partha). Goblins enter the caverns searching for hidden treasures and fighting with the dwarves who guard them. Tunnels can speed the goblins; death traps can kill them. All characters are metal figures. Two players.

CAVERNS OF DOOM (Heritage USA). Enter a series of caverns in search of treasures of all kinds. A die calls up monsters (which, like the adventurers, are metal figures to be colored with paints supplied) and governs their attacks. One to 6 players.

COSMIC ENCOUNTER (Eon Products).

Alien cultures attempt to invade their neighbors' planets. Results depend on the forces committed, including allies who can be persuaded to join, the choice of "challenge" cards, and the unique power of each culture. Two to 4 players; up to 8 with expansion kits.

CREATURE THAT ATE SHEBOYGAN, THE (SPI). One player chooses a monster and secretly endows it with various strengths and special abilities to wreak death and destruction. The other sets up police and national guard units to defend the city. Two players.

CRYPT OF THE SORCERER (Heritage USA). Similar to Caverns of Doom, but smaller. The two can be combined for a giant adventure. One to 4 players.

CYTEARIANS (Creative Prototypes Corporation). Travel through space, mining minerals and then selling them at special stations. The quantity of minerals available, power used, selling price, and actions of hostile aliens are all set by cards. Two to 4 players.

DARKOVER (Eon Products). A struggle to capture the central castle, gaining power from holding outer ones. Battle by choosing one of three "power discs": Keeper, which beats Starstone, which beats Sword, which beats Keeper. The loser can seek revenge with a psychic spell. Four players.

DEMONLORD (Heritage USA). A "small" game with a limited number of army and character counters. But a lot can happen, including the use of magic in battle, the winning over of neutrals, and much more. Two players.

DIMENSION DEMONS (Metagaming). The halves of the board represent different dimensions for demons and humans. Demons transport by picking a target hex but dice throws can send them off.

Humans can only transport after capturing a machine from the demons. Two players.

DUNGEON! (TSR). A simple introduction to fantasy gaming. Players choose their adventurer type and enter the dungeon in search of treasure. The deeper they go, the greater the value but the more fearsome the monsters. Two to 8 players.

FAMOUS MONSTERS (Heritage USA). Humans enter young Dr. Frankenstein's castle in an attempt to rescue Elsa from an assorted group of monsters. All are represented by metal figures that can be decorated with supplied paints. Two players.

INTRUDER (Task Force). An alien being is brought to a space station. Innocent at first, it develops into more and more of a threat, as the crew attempts to contain and then to kill it. A limited number of counters, but a lot can happen. One to 3 players.

KUNG FU 2100 (Steve Jackson Games). Hand to hand combat, and also feet. Some weapons are involved, as the "terminators" attempt to wipe out all traces of the "clonemaster." One or two players.

MERLIN (Heritage USA). An intense battle-to-the-death between Merlin and Morgana le Fay, each able to call on magical powers and three helpers. The eight metal figures can be colored with the paint supplied. Two players.

*MYSTIC WOOD, THE (Ariel/Fantasy Games Unlimited). A hidden wood is set up with two gates, a tower, and forty-two face-down cards. Knights explore by turning up an adjacent card. They discover objects and denizens, who can be helpful or hostile. Two to 4 players.

OUTPOST GAMMA (Heritage USA). A fight on a small planet far in the future. A small number of "Legionnaires" use advanced weapon technology in an attempt to subdue the native hordes. Moving "energy storms" disrupt the weapons. Two players.

SAGA (TSR). Viking heroes, in search of glory, slay monsters and start kingdoms. The dice throw for settling combat can be modified by runes, gods, spells, magic items, and luck points. Two to 6 players.

SECOND EMPIRE (Dimenson Six Enterprises). Using a stock of raw materials, each player constructs his own space navy. The ships are sent into space to do battle and to search for raw materials and the lost technologies of the first empire. Two to 4 players.

*SORCERER'S CAVE, THE (Ariel/Fantasy Games Unlimited). A huge cave of many levels is built by placing large cards one at a time. As players explore the cave, another set of cards indicates hazards, treasures, and creatures that can be hostile or friendly. One to 4 players.

SPELLBINDER (Task Force). Small armies battle in the usual manner. However, each is led by a wizard who can cast powerful spells but must husband his "spellbinder points" carefully. Two to 4 players.

SURVIVAL/THE BARBARIAN (Task Force).

Two different games are supplied. In the first, from one to six survivors of a crashed spaceship try to reach the research station, fighting animals and each other along the way. In the second, one or two barbarians search for an ancient sword and shield.

THEY'VE INVADED PLEASANTVILLE (TSR). The alien attempts to take over the residents, keeping the "zombies" secret as long as possible. The town player tries to convince the residents that the alien exists, rescue the zombies, and locate the alien leader. Two players.

VAMPYRE (TSR). Search for Dracula's coffins on a map of Transylvania, but beware of becoming a werewolf by being bitten twice! For the extended game, flip the board and try to destroy Dracula in his castle. Two to 6 players.

WITCH'S CALDRON (Ral Partha). The wizard, with ten adventurers, enters the witch's lair in search of treasure and magic weapons. There they battle the witch and her eight gruesome servants. All characters are metal figures. Two players.

WIZARD'S QUEST (Avalon Hill). The spaces on an island are filled with the players' "men," nasty little "orcs," and three treasures for each—placed by opponents in hard-to-reach locations. Players establish kingdoms, do battle, and win by retrieving their treasures. Two to 6 players.

SPORTS GAMES.

ACROSS THE BOARD (MPH). Players bid for eleven horses, numbered from 2 to 12. In a race they advance when their number is thrown, with some control by the thrower. Bets and payoffs are handled with a simple, but ingenious, device. Three or more players.

ALL-AMERICAN FOOTBALL (Cadaco). Offensive player secretly chooses a play, represented by a disc divided into sections. Defensive player chooses a disc that he feels will counter the chosen play. Both are inserted into spinners, which determine the result. Two players.

ALL STAR BASEBALL (Cadaco). Uses a spinner, but discs with divisions representing the batting averages of actual players are inserted for each spin. A batting order is set up for each team. Two players.

BASEBALL (Jax Limited). Start by throwing a die with two sides each of Strike, Ball, and Play. If Play shows before a strikeout or base on balls, three regular dice are thrown. The result is read on a chart for the number of men on base. One or more players.

BOWL AND SCORE (Milton Bradley). Throw ten special dice. Faces showing bowling pins represent those left standing. They are then thrown a second time in an attempt to make a "spare." Any number of players.

BRETT BALL (Raymond O. Keltner, M.D.). A clever set of player chips and tables allows for just about every strategic option in baseball. As one example, after a dice throw indicates a "strike" the batter can swing, with success depending on the type of pitch and the batter's strength. Two players.

BUSINESSMAN'S BASEBALL (Fun & Games). Buy managers, star pitchers, star sluggers, ordinary players, or even rookies. A game is played by dice throws and card draws, but winning is not as important as earnings for no-hit innings, strikeouts, hits, etc. Two players.

DOUBLE-PLAY BASEBALL (Lakeside). Nine dice represent hitters of different powers and each player sets up a batting

order. The pitcher throws a die with "ball" on two faces and "good pitch" on the others. After the latter, the batter's die determines the result. Two players.

FAST-BREAK BASKETBALL (Lakeside). Three dice for each player represent their center, forward, and guard. Numbers and symbols on the dice translate the throws, usually one by each player, into action on the court. Two players.

GOLF RUMMY (Allpaul, Inc./Just Games). From a hand of seven cards, players choose the best "clubs," depending on the yards to reach the hole. Drawing hole-in-one or hazard cards can help or hinder. Two or 3 players, or 4 with an extra deck.

HALF-TIME FOOTBALL (Lakeside). Six special dice provide for a simple fast-moving contest. Two players.

HEAVYWEIGHT BOXING (Excalibre Games). Actual boxers are represented by cards rating six different characteristics. In an exchange (three to a round) the chosen stance for each boxer, plus one or more die throws, also influence the results. Two players.

NECK AND NECK (Yaquinto). Players can secretly bet on one or more of the six horses in a race. The throw of two dice tells which horse can be moved and the distance. But a player can refuse to move the horse. Two to 6 players.

"PRO" BASEBALL CARD GAME (Just Games). By drawing cards, almost all plays are covered. Two players.

PRO FOTO-FOOTBALL (Cadaco). One player chooses an offense (a card with a jagged line), inserts it in a holder and pegs it in one of five positions. The other chooses a defense (a transparent card with tacklers, etc.) and places it above. As the holder is pulled away the play unfolds.

RACETRACK (EHP). Players secretly draw cards to indicate which horses will win points for them. Then a race is run, players throwing the dice and moving the horse matching the number on one die the distance of the other. Two to 6 players.

REGATTA (Avalon Hill). A game of skill in which players maneuver their sailboats so as to take every advantage of the wind. Positioning of markers and islands allows an endless variety of courses to be set up. Two to 6 players.

RUNNER'S WORLD MARATHON GAME (Tega). The opportunity to vary one's pace—from walk to sprint—adds strategic options to this realistic version of the popular race. Two to 6 players.

SOCCER (EHP). A simple but visually satisfying simulation. Dice throws are used freely to move any number of men or to pass the ball. A count of

seven is needed to steal the ball. Two players.

SOCCER STARS (Sol-Tec). On a field of many squares, players move their men and dribble the ball. To pass, a target space is chosen. A spinner then indicates if the pass is on target or how far off it is, longer passes going farther astray. Two players.

SPARE-TIME BOWLING (Lakeside). Similar to Bowl and Score.

SPEED CIRCUIT (Avalon Hill). A realistic game of auto racing on three actual tracks. Drawing cards give each car different specifications, which must be used skillfully in order to win. In the advanced game players design their own cars. Two to 6 players.

TRIPLE CROWN (Lakeside). A race where you can bet on your horse to win, place, or show. In moving you can choose a fast, medium, or slow die, possible winnings depending on the choice. Two to 4 players.

MISCELLANEOUS "IMITATION OF LIFE" GAMES.

AIRWAYS (MJC Inc./National Games). Players race from Miami to Seattle, choosing their paths through airports of the United States. A spinner gives clearances for take-off and for landing. Travel between cities is done by acquiring digit counters matching the listed mileage. Two to 4 players.

APACHE (Yaquinto). One or two players represent the Whites who attempt to settle the West and construct a railroad. One to four players are Indians who try to hinder this by sneak attacks. Two to 6 players.

ART GAME, THE (Bancroft Darrow).

Players circle the board, attempting to get works of art—attractive pictures are supplied—into complete sets, which increase their value. Sales between players are negotiated or set by a "markup" die. Two to 4 players.

ASSASSIN! (Southold Game Corporation). Players move along a path of cities, buying and selling seven types of illicit commodities. In certain situations a player may hire an assassin to get rid of an opponent. The higher the price, the greater the chance of success! Two to 4 players.

BARGAIN HUNTER (Milton Bradley). Move

around the board to fill a shopping list of nineteen items. Although completing first is essential, it often pays to wait for a better price since raising money can take time. Charge purchases must be approved by a machine. Two to 4 players.

BEVERLY HILLS (Jax Limited). Roam by dice throw through all the elegant neighborhoods. Receive money, mainly by drawing the right cards. Spend the money at Gucci, Tiffany's, etc. to gain status points. Two to 6 players.

BLACKOUT, THE POWER GAME (Kirkland Game Company). A combination of moving along an outer track by die throw and building a network of power plants on an inner grid. Spaces on the track cause exchanges of money and allow power plants to be built, upgraded, or taken over. Two to 4 players.

BOUNTY HUNTER (Nova Game Designs). A very novel game of gunfighting in the Old West. Each player uses a book of 290 pictures showing an individual's view. As players move they are directed to new pages, cleverly coordinated to keep the proper relationships. Two to 10 players.

*CAREERS (Parker Brothers). Players choose some combination of Money, Fame and Happiness as their goal and try to achieve it in one or more of eight careers. Move by dice, but "Opportunity" and "Experience" cards allow for skillful play. Two to 6 players.

CIVILIZATION (Avalon Hill). A massive game in which civilizations start from a single token, grow, build cities, trade, fight, develop art and technology, and win by reaching a certain level. Seven players, down to 2.

COMPULSION (Edventure). Move by dice throw along the "real life" path where money comes fairly slowly and steadily, or switch to the "track" and gamble for the big bucks. Players can negotiate deals, particularly when one lands on a space allowing a free move. Two to 6 players.

CONSPIRACY (Milton Bradley). A different kind of game, where players make secret payoffs to eight spies in an effort to bring a briefcase to their headquarters. Moves can be challenged and an informer can eliminate another spy. Three or 4 players.

CREDIT ABILITY (The Ungame Company). Players draw secret objectives. These tell how many credit cards are required and which type of items to buy with them. As players land on various spaces they must balance the urge to buy against their cash position. Two to 6 players.

DALLAS (Yaquinto). Members of the Ewing family amass fortunes by using "event" cards, by gaining control of corporations, and particularly by being elected president at family meetings. Votes come from stock holdings, proxies, bargaining, and blackmail. Two to 7 players.

1829 (Hartland Trefoil/The Games People Play). A very detailed simulation of the growth of railroads in England. Much equipment is provided and the rules are rather extensive. Players can start with the "Simple" game and then go through the "Intermediate" to the "Full" game. Two to 9 players.

ENERGY SYSTEMS (McJay Game Company). Players choose an energy system, from electric, the cheapest, to solar, the most expensive. They can also invest in various energy-saving devices. A four-year path is traversed, with expenses lower for those who invested more. Two to 4 players.

EXCUSES, EXCUSES (Waddingtons). Starts with a race to the office, using cards and a die to make progress and hinder opponents. Player must face the boss and supply acceptable excuses. Two to 6 players.

EXPEDITION (The Kirk Game Company). An attractive reenactment of the early search for the treasures of Egypt. Cards picturing actual objects are discovered and, for major finds, put together for a high score. Two to 6 players.

FRONTIER–6 (Rimbold Enterprises). Adventures in the Old West: from farming and ranching through banking and gold prospecting to rustling, robbing a bank, and bounty-hunting. Attractive equipment provided to keep track of it all. Two to 6 players.

GENERAL HOSPITAL, THE GAME OF (Cardinal). Up to ten participate, preferably an even number of each sex. Character sheets list points players gain or lose in various ways, such as romance, power, etc. Board spaces and cards are important, but there is constant opportunity for player interaction.

HOSTAGE (Pik VI Games). Each player attempts to collect six cards in proper order, representing the steps in resolving a hostage situation. Cards are obtained by landing on board spaces and by negotiating with opponents. Two to 4 players.

IRS GAME, THE (EHP). Players choose from Tax Deduction cards of five types, from "fraudulent" where they collect a lot, to "innocent" where they actually pay. If called to an "audit" their last card is subjected to the reading on a spinner. Innocence is rewarded and guilt punished—but not always. Two to 4 players.

ITINERARY (Xanadu Leisure, Ltd.). Airports of the world are arranged in clusters, with traveling paths between. Movement is by dice throw, but there are constant choices to be made: which of three destinations to head for; when to change planes; whether to block an opponent; etc. Two to 5 players.

JUNTA (Creative Wargames Workshop). In a vote where influence cards are used and positions are promised, one player is chosen as president of a corrupt country. Then budgets dividing the spoils are voted. Players can offer bribes, hire assassins, start coups, and more. Two to 7 players.

LAND GRAB (Waddingtons). Starting with limited funds, players buy land and construct small buildings which bring in income. Later they erect more profitable buildings on new land and land cleared by demolition. Dealing between players is allowed. Two to 4 players.

LIFE, THE GAME OF (Milton Bradley). Spin the wheel and travel along the path of life in an automobile on an elaborate three-dimensional board. There are some decisions to be made but luck is the predominant factor. Two to 9 players.

LOVE BOAT WORLD CRUISE GAME, THE (The Ungame Company). As a star passenger you have opportunities to draw or decline cards at different ports or for various on-board activities. Since there is a maximum holding, you try for those advantageous to your character. Familiarity with the cards helps. Two to 6 players.

MID-LIFE CRISIS (The Game Works). The many board spaces and cards take you through the ages from thirty to fifty-five. Players try for the most money, the least stress and the fewest divorce points. But one player can win by going broke, cracking up, and breaking up. Two to 6 players.

MONEY TALKS (REH/Art Fair). This is a strange one, covering all aspects of money and life. Among the things that can happen, a player in debt can sell his spouse or children, and a "rip-off" space allows taking all of one opponent's property or cash. One to 4 players.

MOVIE GAME, THE (The Movie Game, Limited). Players move between two tracks in search of a writer, producer, director, star, and studio deal. They then jet to a third track for film distribution in three countries. The player reaching "box office" still in possession of all of these wins. Two to 4 players.

MOVIE STUDIO MOGUL (International Marketing Consultants). Eight studios, each with a space for a star, director, and writer, are located along a path, together with other spaces. Players acquire personnel by landing or trading. With a set, players can produce up to six movies, each increasing the landing fee. Two to 6 players.

OREGON TRAIL (Fantasy Games Unlimited). Using a large map of the western United States, players are Trail Bosses bringing a party west. Along the way, the Boss must deal with a dangerous environment and potentially hostile Indians. One to 8 players.

ORGANIZED CRIME (Koplow Games). Mobs consist of a boss and twenty men. Men can be assigned to raising money, to corrupting officials or, as hit-men, to protecting their boss and rubbing out

rivals. Meetings of the "National Commission" allow for dealing. Two to 4 players.

ORIGINS OF WORLD WAR II by James Dunnigan (Avalon Hill). Developed from his game in this book. There is the historical version, five "what-if?" scenarios, and a way to play-by-mail. Two to 5 players. Also a classroom game for greater numbers.

OUTDOOR SURVIVAL by James Dunnigan (Avalon Hill). On a hex board representing wilderness terrain of various types, players compete against nature and—depending on which of the five variations is chosen—against each other. Daily water is essential; food less so. One to 4 players.

PAYDAY (Parker Brothers). Moving on a calendar, players collect a salary at the start of a month and pay their bills by the end. Landing on various spaces brings mail, lotteries, welfare, and more. Two to 4 players.

PIRATE (EHP). Players earn Pieces of Eight by using cleverly paired treasure maps, trading between continents, taking a chance on the spinner, or engaging an enemy ship in battle. Two to 4 players.

PRESIDENTIAL CAMPAIGN (Banovac Corporation/John N. Hansen). Move along the "primary" path collecting Election Campaign and Delegate cards. With proper set of ten, move on to "election" path. Another set allows a try for the presidency, throwing dice against top contender. Two to 6 players.

PRIVATEER (Scott Peterson/Discovery Games). The attractive cloth board has a treasure island in the center and harbors in the corners. Players use dice throws to move one or two of their three ships. Object is to pick up a "purse" and bring it safely home. Two to 4 players.

PROFIT FARMING (Foster Enterprises). Action is primarily determined by landing on spaces and by drawing cards. But players make choices between used or new farm equipment, between paying the bank for services or a lesser amount to an opponent, and when to buy or sell land. Two to 6 players.

PURELY ACADEMIC (Tag Enterprises/National Games). Reach a building in the college town by exact throw and pick up a "requirement" card, often with a surprise—pleasant or not so. Requirements run from "Bar" through "Sororities & Frats" to some that are slightly scholarly. Two to 8 players.

RAIL BARON (Avalon Hill). Players move along actual U.S. rail lines, collecting money for reaching a destination city. Rail lines are purchased and opponents must pay to use them. More powerful engines allow for extra dice throws. Two to 6 players.

RAILS THROUGH THE ROCKIES (Adventure Games). Railroad construction circa 1880 is covered in considerable, but not overwhelming, detail. A player's lines are marked with wax crayon on an erasable plastic board. Two to 6 players.

RATRACE (Waddingtons). Players start in the working class, and by fortunate throws of the dice advance through the middle class and into high society. They acquire status symbols and win by retiring with a tidy sum. Two to 6 players.

REAL ESTATE, THE GAME OF (Char-Donn/CPM). Drive around neighborhoods of varying affluence gaining listings of houses for sale. Try to match your own or opponents' prospects with listings. Collect commissions if mortgage goes through. Two to 4 players.

ROARING 20's, THE (Yaquinto). Players are crime bosses who try to pull off a "Big Job" and get back to a "Hideout;" each location is set by cards. Players take turns as the "Police Commissioner," who can chase the bosses or accept a bribe. Two to 6 players.

SALVATION! (Omni House). Stay on the "straight and narrow" and earn an occasional "merit." Or go "out in the world" for more merits, but also the danger of getting some nasty money. Merits are placed in the players' mail boxes, for delivery to heaven. Two to 4 players.

SKI GAME, LE (John N. Hansen). Moving along a path by die throw, players earn money, buy equipment of varying quality, gain experience, and finally enter a "pro-race." The points earned depend on players' equipment, experience, and luck. Two to 6 players.

SPACE SHUTTLE 101 (The Ungame Company). Leave Earth for missions in space. Six "propellant" and four "consumable" units are carried. Return at any time and score for missions completed multiplied by remaining units, but score nothing if either type runs out. Two to 4 players.

SPIES (SPI). Secrets are hidden in many cities of Europe and spies are sent to find and return them to a player's capital. Counterspies and police can capture spies, but "action chits" of various kinds afford protection. Two to 5 players.

STICK THE IRS (Courtland Playthings). Invest in "tax shelters" that can pay off or cost, depending on a die throw. But they do provide a "write-off" when tax is due. Pay the IRS half of all unprotected income each time around the board. Two to 6 players.

STOLITICS (Pelican Studios). Players start as Junior Executives and fight their way to Chairman of the Board, bumping opponents along the way. To advance a notch a certain stock holding is required, but often stock must be sold to raise money. Two to 4 players.

SUE AND COUNTER-SUE (McDaniel Brothers). Players have opportunities to sue opponents for what they think they can get. The suit can be negotiated, or can be settled by a dice throw. There can also be countersuits, bribes, appeals (where the other players are the jury) and more. Two to 6 players.

SURFING, THE GAME OF (Cra-Mor). Be the first to reach "Super Khuna." Special dice, three spinners, and three decks of cards can keep you moving on one turn—but backward as well as forward. Two to 4 players.

SURVIVE! (Parker Brothers). Hexagon pieces are used to build an island on the board. Players place people of varying value on the island. The island dis-

integrates one piece at a time as players try to rescue their people from many hazards. Two to 4 players.

THAT'S SHOW BIZ! (Giordano-Wettrau Enterprises). Move around the board earning money for lessons in tap, ballet, jazz, voice, and acting. Audition by drawing three cards from a pack with three of each talent. If your lessons match, you win. Two to 4 players.

TRUST ME (Parker Brothers). Twelve briefcases are secretly loaded with contents of varying worth and then placed around the board. As players bring them back to the center, they try to talk the others into investing, especially if it is a stinker. Two to 4 players.

VOYAGE TO CIPANGU (Cipangu Game Company/John N. Hansen). An uncharted sea is set up with face down tiles. These are turned as ships reach them. Cipangu is a particular goal, but gold can be earned—or lost—in other ways, including piracy. Most gold in home port at turn of last tile wins. Two to 4 players.

HUMOROUS GAMES—*where the theme can be more important than the play.*

BUREAUCRACY (Avalon Hill). Players attempt to become a Director in the federal civil service, operating as a "lifer," an "over achiever," an "empire builder," or a "hustler." Progress takes place on a massive board with the help of six decks of cards. Two to 8 players.

CHUTZPAH (Cadaco). Use false teeth, hot dogs, and other wacky tokens to move around a gag-filled board, buying mink stoles, having your teeth capped, and

arranging for daughter Shirley's catered wedding. Two to 6, or 8 players.

FIX OR REPAIR DAILY (EHP). Gas stations and repair shops are bought to collect from opponents. Trading to get more of the same type ups the price. Landing on an opponent causes an expensive accident. Last to go broke wins. Two to 4 players.

FUNNY BONES (Parker Brothers). "The knee bone's connected to the shin bone," or at least it should be in this game where couples win by placing and holding the greatest number of jumbo cards between their proper bones. Two or more couples.

GAS CRISIS (McJay Game Company). One thousand gallons of gasoline are needed for a trip around the board. A player stuck with a gas guzzler uses three dice instead of one. Prices rise from $1.00 to $500.00 and players drop out as they go broke. Two to 6 players.

GO FOR BROKE (Selchow & Righter). Win by being lucky enough to lose $1,000,000 in unlucky encounters with roulette, the races, the stock market, and others. Played on a board using dice and a special spinner. Two to 5 players.

LIE CHEAT & STEAL (Paragon-Reiss). As players pick up money to buy votes they can lie about a drawn "$" card, and collect unless challenged. "Black eye" cards allow an opponent to be blackmailed, but a bluffer can be hit by a libel suit. Two to 6 players.

PETER PRINCIPLE GAME, THE (Avalon Hill). A business game where you try your best *not* to advance from Assistant to President, even if this means committing suicide by attempting a "Peter's parry." Last player surviving wins. Two to 4 players.

PUBLIC ASSISTANCE (Hammerhead Enterprises). Start as an "able-bodied welfare recipient" and keep collecting money as the dice take you around. With luck you get extra cash for crime and for each illegitimate child. With bad luck you get sent to the worker's path, and even worse to a union job. Two to 4 players.

SCHNOZZLE GAME (Opec, Inc.). Using two tankers each, players sail through the Strait of Hokum, the Perishable Gulf, and other well-known waterways in a race to obtain oil from six different sources. Two to 4 players.

PSYCHOLOGICAL GAMES—*which in some way are tied in with personality and analysis.*

ETHICS (Art Fair). A player draws one of thirty "situation cards," each presenting a moral dilemma. Modifiers to the situation can also come into play. The others rate the player on his decision, and how well he defends it. Up to 8 players.

INTUITION (Tech Games). One player announces a "self-portrait," an "ideal," or an "image" and then secretly chooses ten from a set of thirty cards with descriptive characteristics. The others place cards from identical sets, the score depending on how closely they match. Two to 4 players.

REUNION (The Ungame Company). Not a game, but an opportunity to relate to one of a number of pictures, to imagine a happening, to use your intuition, or to recall a childhood memory. Two to 6 "players."

SHRINK (Art Fair). Not a competitive game, but rather an opportunity for self-discovery. Forty-seven cards have pictures of various animals, objects, styles, etc. Players choose those that fit them, that they'd like to be, or not to be. Two or more players.

SOCIAL SECURITY (The Ungame Company). No competition involved. Instead a mechanism for getting three to six participants, especially family members, to look at the other's ideas and feelings—and at their own.

UNGAME, THE (The Ungame Company). As the name implies not a game at all, but a mechanism for getting three to six participants to start communicating. If played honestly, each can learn a lot about the others, and about himself.

DEDUCTIVE GAMES—*where the object is to discover something that is hidden.*

*CLUEDO (Parker Brothers). A murder is set up by secretly removing a suspect, weapon, and room card from a special deck. The remainder are dealt out. Using a little luck, good play, and logical deduction, players try to discover the three original cards. Three to 6 players.

GUESS WHO? (Lakeside). Pictures of twenty-four people are mounted on racks so that each can be turned down. Questions about characteristics of the opponent's chosen person allow groups to be eliminated. Correct identification wins. Two players.

HOAX (Eon Products). Players are dealt an identity card from a deck containing two each of the following characters: King, Judge, Vicar, Wizard, Thief, Peasant. Each has a particular power, but players can—indeed must —bluff by claiming other powers. Three to 8 players.

JOTTO (Selchow & Righter). A game of deductive logic as one player tries to discover, by the proper choice of test words, a five-letter word chosen by the other. Two players.

*MASTERMIND (Pressman). One player secretly sets up a row of four colored pegs. The other player sets up a row and is graphically informed how many are of matching color and how many are in, and not in, proper position. One point is scored for each trial until the solution.

PROBE (Parker Brothers). Each player places a secret word of from four to twelve letters in a rack. Score for discovering letters in an opponent's word and higher for the last letter. An "activity deck" can help or hinder. Two to 4 players.

PROSPECTOR GAME, THE (McJay Game Company). A simple mystery is set up by removing a "prospector" and a "strike" card from sets of eight. Players land on spaces that allow them to pick up cards and also to question opponents about cards they hold. Two to 6 players.

RUNES (Eon Products). Each letter of the alphabet is broken down into "runesticks" of four basic shapes. Players choose words and then gain information about the opponents' by checking whether a particular runestick is part of a particular letter. Two to 4 players, and a different solitaire.

SLEUTH by Sid Sackson (Avalon Hill).

Thirty-six cards, each with a different combination of three elements: Gem, Type, Color. A mystery card is removed and the rest are dealt out. Cards from another deck allow various kinds of questions about an opponent's holdings. Three to 7 players.

221B Baker Street. (John N. Hansen). A mystery read from a "case" card directs players to fourteen London locations, where they pick up clues. But hints can inform them that certain clues are not needed. Twenty cases are included, and supplements are available. Two to 6 players.

RACE GAMES—*from the simple to the complex.*

Pachisi, which has a long history in India, is the model for many race games. It is played on a cross-shaped board, each player having four men. Using dice, men are entered on a path, travel around it, and move to safety in the center. A single man, when hit by an enemy, must start over.

Aggravation (Lakeside). Similar to Pachisi except that the board has been expanded to allow for play by from 2 to 6 players. (Some editions can only be played by up to 4.)

Backgam III (EHP). Like Backgammon, except that there are a number of different paths. Men when taken off are not reentered, and chips can be picked up that earn extra points if carried to the goal. Two players.

Bottleneck (Ideal). Something like Backgammon, but much tighter as the six pieces of each team pass and capture along a single track. One die limits the pieces that can be moved, another the distance. Two players.

Counterstrike (Essex Games). Similar to Backgammon, but players move in the same direction along an eighteen-space track. A stack of two men can be captured by two enemies moved together. Points are scored for men in ad-

vanced positions, one hundred winning. Two players.

Dice-Gammon (Boardgame Mania). Backgammon played with dice instead of the usual pieces. Each time a die is moved it takes the value of the spaces moved. A space is won by having a higher point count, and equal point counts can share a space. Two players.

Doubletrack (Milton Bradley). The race takes place on the inner track, but what happens is controlled by spaces along the outer track. Movement here is by dice throw, but opportunities arise for making strategic choices and arranging deals. Three or 4 players.

Hare & Tortoise (Waddingtons). Despite rather juvenile graphics, this race game is almost completely one of skill. Carrots are the means of moving forward, the amount increasing rapidly for each space. New ones are obtained by falling back or by being in the right space at the right time. Two to 4 players.

King Tut's Game (Cadaco). A race to bring five men to the end of a thirty-space track. Special dice (or staves in the deluxe edition) allow moves from zero to four. Congestion along the track can force backward moves. Two players.

PARCHEESI (Selchow & Righter). Very close to classic Pachisi. Published for over one hundred years. Two to 4 players.

PASSING THROUGH THE NETHERWORLD (Kirk Game Company). The ancient Egyptian race along a path of thirty spaces. The board is attractively illustrated, the pieces and throwsticks are authentic, and the accompanying book is rich with historical drawings and insights. Two players.

PENUMBRA (Southold Game Corporation). A rather complex race to reach the top of an Aztec pyramid, using men with three different functions. One unique feature is that before a player uses an odd dice throw, the opponent may make defensive moves. Two players.

SHAKESPEARE (Avalon Hill). In the basic version each player races three men by dice throw and directions on the board.

In the tournament versions players get extra moves for knowledge of Shakespeare's plays. One to 4 players.

SHIFTI (Orda/Educational Design, Inc.). A race to move four men along paths from one corner of the board to the other. But the paths constantly change as a dice throw allows a player to shift one of the four levers. Two to 4 players.

*SORRY! (Parker Brothers). A special deck of cards ups the excitement. Men can change places with an opponent, can move backward to avoid a trip around the board, and can be forced out of the safety zone into the path of danger. Two to 4 players.

UR–ROYAL GAME OF SUMER (Selchow & Righter). Each player maneuvers seven wooden men along this reproduction of an ancient board. Certain spaces call for bonuses or penalties, which can set up chain reactions. A turn continues until one dot and two blanks are thrown on the special dice. Two players.

MATCHING GAMES—*where pieces as played must relate to each other in some way.*

COLORMATCH (Ideal). Cards representing a face of a Rubik's Cube are played to a pegged board, and can cover parts of previously placed cards. Score by completing a three by three square of the master color. Two to 6 players.

DOMINGO (Whitman). Square tiles are divided diagonally, the two halves having from zero to six dots. Players draw tiles and place them on their own boards, trying for a straight line of five tiles that match where they join. One to 4 players.

DOMINIQUE (Samuel Ward). Forty-four

tiles have rows of three circles in different arrangements of four colors. These are played to a four by eleven array. Score for lines of three or more of the same color, double for diagonals. Two to 4 players.

DOTTO (Tega). Fifty-six square tiles are marked with four dots in different combinations of four colors. These are played to a board, scoring for lines of three or more of the same color, diagonals counting double. Two to 6 players.

PUZZLE PERFECTION (Lakeside). The

color showing on the die allows a player to take a piece of that color, usually choosing between varying shapes and sizes. The object is to fill a frame and also to match markings on the pieces. Two to 6 players.

QUAD-OMINOS (Pressman). One hundred and twenty-five square tiles are marked in the corners with numbers from 0 to 5. A tile must be played next to an edge of the previously played tile, with the numbers matching. Two to 8 players.

QUINTILLIONS (Kadon Enterprises). A set of twelve hardwood pieces have all possible arrangements of five cubes connected in one plane. Cut with a laser beam, they fit together precisely for a number of different games and puzzles. One to 4 players.

STACK-OMINOS (Pressman). Transparent squares with from one to six dots in different arrangements are stacked in pockets on the board. No dot may cover another. Score for all dots showing on each pile played to. Two to 4 players.

TRI-OMINOS (Pressman). Fifty-six triangular tiles are marked in the corners with combinations of the numbers 0 to 5. Each piece played must touch an edge of the previously played piece, with the numbers matching. Two to 4 players.

VAGABONDO (Invicta). Plastic pieces of different shapes and in three shades of red or blue are played to a large grid. Pieces of the same shade may not touch. Score for the piece played and all those it touches. Two to 6 players.

ABSTRACT STRATEGY GAMES—*where the outcome depends completely, or almost completely, on skill.*

ANTICIPATION (Lodestone Games). By simple moves or by jumps, players attempt to bring their pieces to a promotion area. Before each turn the opponent can mark the position he believes will be occupied. If correct, the piece starts over. Two players.

AVANTE (Krystoff International). A luxuriously packaged mini-Chess. The board is six by six and each side has six pieces. Except for "Chiefs," opposing pieces of the same rank cannot threaten each other. Two players.

CHINESE CHESS (Gabriel). One player is called "same," the other "different." Both may move a piece of either of the two colors, but same can only jump and capture pieces of the same color, while different can only capture the opposite color.

CONNECT FOUR (Milton Bradley). Checkers are dropped into one of seven vertical columns, each six spaces high. Win by getting four checkers of your color in a row—vertically, horizontally, or diagonally. Two players.

DOMINATION by Sid Sackson (Milton Bradley). This is the new name for Focus (page 125). A molded board with stacking pieces is provided, and I have come up with a "fast" variation playable by two, three, or four.

DOWN THE TUBES (Whitman). Similar to Chinese Checkers except that the pieces are pegs that can be "lost" if they hit a hidden hole. Start with fifteen pegs and win by moving five across. Six movable board pieces make each game different. Two to 6 players.

FORTE (Waddingtons). Players start with seven knights. A knight moves along a path, ending in a fort on either side. Four in a row wins a joust, but the winner uses one less knight in the next. Three jousts wins the tournament. Two players.

GUERILLA (Fantasy Games Unlimited). On a field of many triangles, players build groups by placing pieces on the intersections. Pieces jumping within a group cause movement, with the object of capturing enemy pieces on contact. Two players.

INNER CIRCLE (Milton Bradley). Four hex-shaped cardboard fields are stacked. Pieces move along spaces, attempting to stop in holes. When all holes are filled a field is lifted, removing pieces with it. Player reaching the one hole in the bottom field wins. Two to 4 players.

HEX-MEISTER (John N. Hansen). A battle fought on a board consisting of a central hexagon surrounded by five rings of hexagons. Movement is quite free as long as "gates" are open. Although pieces are captured, the object is to occupy the gates in one line or in one ring. Two players.

INTERMEDIUM (Fantasy Games Unlimited). Piles of pieces are "moved" by placing them one at a time in adjoining spaces. A single piece cannot move. Ending a move on a single piece can lead to enemy captures. Win by immobilizing the enemy or capturing his "city." Two players.

INTERPLAY (Philip Shoptaugh Games). The wooden playing pieces consist of solid cylinders, hollow cylinders, and pegs. The last two, one from each player, can share a hole in the seven by seven array. Players in turn place, or move, a piece. Win with a specific row of five. Two players.

JUXTA (Lodestone Games). The board's spaces are of three different colors. Players have six pieces, two of each color. A player can make a single move or jump his own pieces, but must always land on a matching color. Six versions with varying objectives. Two to 4 players.

KANGAROO (Samuel Ward). Players start with sixteen pegs in holes at the ends of an eight by eight array on a plastic board. Movement is only by a jump or a series of jumps, over friendly or enemy pegs. Enemies are captured. Two players.

KENSINGTON (Samuel Ward). Played on the points of a layout consisting of interlocking shapes. Pieces are first placed and later moved to adjoining points. Surrounding a triangle or square allows relocating of opponent's pieces. Surrounding a hexagon wins. Two players.

KWATRO (Kwatro Corporation/John N. Hansen). Thirty-four spaces are connected by straight and diagonal lines. Players in turn occupy a space. Win with four on a line and no enemy piece between. Two players.

MONEYCHASE (Tomorrow's Games by Rollis). The board is made up of intersecting circles, ellipses, and straight lines and play takes place on the intersections. Most pieces (representing different coins) can sweep around one or more of the paths. Surrounding an area captures an enemy. Two players.

MOONSTAR by Alex Randolph (Avalon Hill). Although dice are used, a game of pure skill. Pieces are placed along a circular path. Dice are thrown, the pieces are moved, one for each die, and score for landing on occupied spaces. Players bid for the right to do the moving. Two or more players.

OH-WAH-REE by Alex Randolph (Avalon Hill). Some new twists to the ancient game of Mancala (see page 40). Two to 4 players.

OTHELLO (Gabriel). This is a revival of a century-old game called Reversi. Pieces with faces of two different colors are used. Players place a piece so as to bracket at least one line of the opponent's color between his own pieces, flipping those bracketed. When board is filled, majority color wins. Two players.

PENTE (Pente Games). In the basic game, two players place stones on the intersections of a large grid. Placing a stone that sandwiches two enemy stones captures them. Win with a row of five, or with ten captured stones. Several variations are given, including play by up to six.

RUBIK'S GAME (Ideal). Using a Rubik's Cube with holes in each square, players in turn place a peg in their color and rotate a segment 90 degrees. Win by getting three pegged squares in a row on any face. Two to 6 players.

QUINTESSENCE (Pentagames). Played on a field of pentagonal spaces, cleverly supplemented by diamond-shaped barriers to create paths. Although a die sets a player's move, the use of "go-again" spaces, "power" spaces, color cards collected in sets, and much more makes this a game of skill. Two to 5 players.

ROUND BOUT (Samuel Ward). On a circular board, an attacker with seven pieces attempts to reach the center against a defender with four pieces. Capture is by jumping. Two players.

SCORE FOUR (Lakeside). A three-dimensional Tic Tac Toe, achieved by placing beads on sixteen upright rods. First four-in-a-row wins, or place all sixty-four beads and score for each row. Two players.

SEEJEH (Leisure Learning Products). Players place pieces on a seven by seven grid until only the center is empty. Pieces move one space orthogonally into an empty space. A bracketed enemy piece is captured and the player can move again. Two players.

SERAUQS (Competitive Games). Each player has four pieces which move on a four by four board, with the object of forming a straight line or a square. But one piece of each team is "wild" and can be used in the opponent's winning position. Two players.

SLIDE 5 (Milton Bradley). Players in turn enter a piece of their color in one of ten grooves, five each at right angles to each other. Pieces already in the groove can be moved and one may be ejected. Five in a row wins. Two players.

SPY FIVE-O (Orda/Educational Design, Inc.). Each player has five secret pieces that have different maximum moves, and values if they reach the goal. The "spy" is slow, but the only piece that can make a capture, and the most valuable. Two players.

SUDDEN SCORE (Samuel Ward). The pieces have "O" for offensive on one side and "X" for defensive on the other. On a turn a player may flip and then move. O pieces move further and can "capture" in a novel manner. X pieces are safe. Win by moving seven pieces into opponent's goal. Two players.

SUPER-SEIZURE (Samuel Ward). Like

Checkers, except that each set has four each of three colors. Each color is prohibited from jumping one of the other colors. A jump can end on an enemy piece of a permitted color, capturing it too. Win by moving across. Two players.

TACTICUBE (Samuel Ward). A colorful cube has a square of nine peg holes on each face. Markings between the holes indicate how diagonal lines wrap around the edges. Rules for five games, roughly based on two-dimensional ones, are given. Two to 4 players.

TOUCH DOWN (Invicta). Forty-nine pegs are mounted in a plastic board. There are ten each of two colors and the rest are "neutral." After the first peg, players in turn press down a peg next to the one just pressed. Object is to down all of your color. Two players.

TOUCHÉ (Gabriel). The transparent pieces contain magnets, red on one side and white on the other. Strips with magnets (which can be rearranged for each game) may cause the pieces to change color with each move. Four in a row wins. Two players.

TOURNAMENT STADIUM CHECKERS (Schaper). The playing field consists of an outer fixed ring, nine rotatable rings, and a fixed central area. As a player rotates a ring, marbles, his own or opponents', move down through aligned slots toward various goals. Two to 4 players.

TRAX (Excalibre Games). Sixty-four tiles are provided. On one face the edges are joined by crossing straight lines, one

black and one white. On the other face the edges are joined by curved lines. Win with a "loop" or a "line" of your color. Two players.

TRECKERS (Yorel Game Company). Checkers for two or three on a roughly triangular board. Five different levels of play are given, the fifth one approaching Chess in complexity.

TURNABOUT (Mag-Nif). Thirty-two square tiles have the edges joined by two crossing lines on one face and by two curved lines on the other. These are placed on an eight by eight grid, one player attempting to link two sides, the other to prevent it.

TWIXT by Alex Randolph (Avalon Hill). Object is to connect your two sides of the board while stopping the opponent. Pegs are placed in turn, and when two of your color are a knight's move apart, they are linked with a plastic bridge. Two or 4 players.

VIS-À-VIS (Selchow & Righter). Twenty-five attractive discs, in five colors, are placed in a grab bag. One player draws one at a time and places it on a five by five board. After each placement the other player may move one disc, attempting to form symmetrical patterns. Score for these, and reverse roles.

WATCH by Claude Soucie (MPH). A new board is created for each game by placing colored discs on a grid. Each time a player moves his man the disc is removed, contracting the board. Win by landing on your opponent or on a disc of the same color he is on. Two players.

WORD GAMES (part I)—*where cards with letters, or letter combinations, are used to form words.*

BALI (Avalon Hill). Played with 108 letter cards in a manner similar to solitaire with regular cards. Since words can be formed in stages, very long ones can be made, with appropriate rewards. But beware, a group can be stolen. One to 4 players.

LEXICON (Waddingtons). Using fifty-two letter cards, the object is to be the first to play out a hand into a crossword layout. Other players are penalized for remaining cards. Two to 6 players; also two solitaires.

QUE (Knots). As well as cards with letters, the double deck has thirty cards with two-letter combinations and two wild cards. Rules for a number of different games are given. One to 8 players.

ROYALTY (S.J. Miller). Players meld words from cards in their hand and opponents have one chance to add a letter or letters to steal the word. Half the 106 cards are black, half red, and words of one color score double. One or more players.

SUM-WORDS (MPH). Letter cards contain only consonants, players choosing their own vowels. Make words from five hand cards and top of discard pile. Younger players can be allowed to score for shorter words. One to 5 players.

WORD RUMMY (Gabriel). Working from a hand of seven cards, players can meld a word or can steal one from an opponent by adding one or more letters to form a new word. Two to 4 players, or up to 8 with a double deck.

WORD GAMES (part II)—*where letter cubes are thrown and words formed from the letters that turn up.*

ADDICTION (Waddingtons). Choose a letter cube, push it down an incline and place it in a five by five grid. Continue with twelve more, forming words in crossword fashion. One or more players.

*BOGGLE (Parker Brothers). Sixteen letter cubes are shaken into a square. Players list words they find by going from letter to letter in any direction. At the end of a time limit, duplicates are eliminated and players score for remaining words, plus length bonuses. Two to 6 players.

CROSS-CUBES (Baron Scott). Shake six black cubes into place on a five by five field. Then throw nineteen cubes with letter faces and, working against a timer, fill them into the field to form a crossword puzzle. One or more players.

CROSSWORD CUBES GAME (Selchow & Righter). Each player is allowed from two to four tosses of fourteen cubes. Forming words in crossword style, he can score for one, and only one, word of each length from two to eight letters. One or more players.

KEEP QUIET (Kopptronix). Played with a

timer, a shaker, and fourteen letter cubes. The letters, however, are in sign language. The basic game calls for words in crossword fashion. One variation rewards the longest word. One or more players.

PERQUACKEY (Lakeside). Players in turn throw ten cubes (thirteen later in the game) and form words, working against a timer. Not more than five words of any one length can be scored. Two or more players.

SPILL & SPELL (Parker Brothers). Although the letters are placed in crossword fashion, the scoring encourages the formation of long words rather than a compact pattern of crossing words. Played with fifteen cubes. One or more players.

WORD YAHTZEE (Milton Bradley). Seven dice have letters, valued from 10 for a "Z" down to 1. Players throw the dice and can rethrow any number twice. Score in categories such as two to seven letter words, all consonants, all vowels, and others. One to 4 players.

WORD GAMES (part III)—*where various types of equipment are employed for forming words out of letters.*

CROSSWORD BINGO (Samuel Ward). Each player takes a "Bingo" card showing twenty letters. Then, working with their own letter tiles, all players attempt to form words before a timer runs out. Matching letters are moved to the card. Continue until one card is filled. Two to 20 players.

CROSSWORD/DOMINOES (Selchow & Righter). Fifty Domino shaped tiles are used, each with two letters, arranged horizontally on one face and vertically on the other. From a hand of five tiles players build interlocking words. Two to 4 players.

CROZZLE (Cadaco). Using sheets of paper inserted into special holders, players construct mini-crossword puzzles. Letters, which all must enter, are called one at a time. Score for all words formed. Two to 4 players.

DIG-IT! (Cadaco). Turn a card and dig into a pile of letters to form a descriptive word to go with it—all working at the same time. First to complete five

cards collects points from the others. Two to 10 players.

GRID WORD (Waddingtons). Cards have two-letter combinations leading to each edge. These are played onto a grid so that wherever two cards are next to each other a proper four-letter word is formed. One to 6 players.

KEEP QUIET REWORD (Kopptronix). Cards are played onto a series of four or five compartments to form a word. Then new words are created by covering letters. The cards have regular letters on one face, sign language on the other. One to 6 players.

NEXUS (Lodestone Games). Words are built using tiles, some with letters and others with syllables—these scoring many more points. Several versions are given. In all, words can be expanded; in some, they can be stolen. One to 4 players.

QUIBBLE (Just Games). Ten generously sized wooden sticks have ten letters arranged vertically on each face. These are randomly formed into a square array. Variations range from finding words in a single row, up to the entire array. One or more players.

RAZZLE (Parker Brothers). A carriage holds six letter cubes. From a central position it can be moved three positions in either direction, tumbling the cubes each time. The first to find a word of four or more letters moves one position toward the enemy. Two players.

RSVP (Selchow & Righter). Played on an upright grid. Each in turn can choose any letter and place it in the grid, the letter showing on both sides. Object is to form words on your side while blocking the opponent. Two players.

SCORING ANAGRAMS (Selchow & Righter). Wooden letter tiles have scoring values. These are faced into a "pool" one at a time. Any player can "call" a word. Words can also be stolen by adding one or more letters, changing the meaning. Two or more players.

SCRABBLE (Selchow & Righter). Letter tiles are played on a board in crossword fashion, scoring for the letters played and also for the spaces covered. Undoubtedly the best-known word game of them all. Two to 4 players.

SPELLBOUND (Lakeside). The unit contains eight letter cubes which shake into a vertical column visible from four sides, each calling for a different type of word formation. Players play each side, with time limits. High total score wins. Two to 4 players.

UPPER HAND (Selchow & Righter). Letter tiles are marked with card suits, which greatly increase their value when trump. High bidder sets trump and must win that many "tricks." Words are formed crossword fashion. Higher value than previous word wins a trick; lower loses. Two to 4 players.

WORD GAMES (part IV)—*where word games are played with whole words.*

FACTS IN FIVE (Avalon Hill). Five categories are chosen from cards and five letter tiles are turned up. In five minutes each player tries to write a word for each category, starting with each letter. The pads provide spaces for a unique scoring system. One or more players.

QUIP QUBES (Selchow & Righter). Cubes with words on their faces are thrown and then played to the board in complete sentences, crossword fashion. Score for length of the sentence and covering bonus spaces. Two players or teams.

SENTENCE CUBE GAME (Selchow & Righter). Words are printed on the faces of twenty-one cubes. These are thrown and a player has three minutes to come up with sentences in crossword fashion. One or more players.

SYNTACTICS (Samuel Ward). Word tiles are played as sentences along a recessed path winding toward the center of the board. Crossing sentences can be entered at ten indicated locations. Two to 4 players.

NUMBER GAMES—*in which digits are manipulated in various ways.*

CALL IT! (Ideal). Players in turn drop chips numbered from 1 to 10 into a can. A player "calls" when he believes a target number has been reached, and scores plus or minus depending on the actual total. Two to 6 players.

CRAZE (Craze Productions). All possible numbers that can be reached arthimetically with three dice (1 low and 216 high) are entered into spaces. Players throw three dice and cross off a space. Score one point for each adjacent crossed off space. Wipe off for a new game. One to 5 players.

EQUABLE (John N. Hansen). Using tiles with numbers, operation signs, decimal points, and fraction bars, players form equations crossword fashion on a large grid. Equations in place may be extended or have one side completely replaced. Two to 4 players.

EQUALS (Waddingtons). Number and operation tiles are played to a board in simple equations that mesh in crossword fashion. Score for highest number in equation and the type of operation. Two to 4 players.

EQUATIONS (Wff 'N Proof). Using cubes with numbers and mathematical symbols, the object is to build a valid equation. Start with addition and subtraction. Advanced versions include powers, roots, and more. Two or more players.

KRYPTO (MPH). From a deck of numbered cards, five are dealt face up. A sixth is faced separately as the "objective." All players try to be the first to use the five cards arithmetically to equal the objective. One or more players.

TIGO (Ward & Sons/CPM). Players attempt to arrange four counters with numbers from a set of 1 to 10, and three others with "+", "−" and "×", so that specified answers are reached. Cards set up the problems and a board makes them easy to see. Two to 4 players.

TRIBULATION (Whitman). Pockets on a board are filled with one-digit number squares. A disc with a number from 1 to 50 is drawn, and the first to find a row of three numbers that equals it—by multiplying two and adding or subtracting the third—wins it. Any number of players.

DICE GAMES—*with usual and very unusual cubes.*

CASINO SLOTS (Lakeside). Throw dice with slot machine symbols one at a time, paying for each or stopping after first or second. For third throw player has choice of two dice, depending on the symbol desired for a possible pay-off. Any number of players.

JACKPOT YAHTZEE (Milton Bradley). Each player has five vertical slots with spaces for from one to five tiles. Tiles, with four symbols, are entered as allowed by the throw of four special dice. Score for lines of the same symbol, or for a total of seven or more. Two to 4 players.

KISMET (Lakeside). Players in turn throw five dice and try, by use of skilled judgement, to make high scores in fifteen categories listed on a score sheet. The dice faces have three different colors and "flush" is one of the categories. Any number of players.

PIGMANIA (Recycled Paper Products/ HirchCo). Instead of dice, two pig figures are thrown. These can land in many different positions, each with its own name and score. A player can usually keep throwing, but loses everything if the pigs touch. Two or more players.

7-SPOT YOTT (Samuel Ward). Five dice with card and joker faces are supplied. Player can throw up to three times and then must choose to score in one of twenty-two categories, mostly Poker hands. Any number of players.

TOP DOG (John N. Hansen). Shake twelve dogs out of half a bone. If any are "sitting up" you can score for these, or throw the others again. Player can stop the score after any throw, or lose all if none sit up. Two or more players.

YAHTZEE (Milton Bradley). Similar to Kismet, but without the "flush" category.

CARD GAMES (part I)—*where regular cards are combined with special equipment.*

AUCTION TRIPOLEY (Cadaco). Collect chips from "pots" by playing the matching card or cards. The suit of these "money cards" is chosen by the winner of an auction, held after players see their hands. A "key card," set by dice throw, can win the auction payment. Two to 9 players.

DUO-BRIDGE (Just Games). Bridge for two. The deal is rigged so that the players get the stronger hands. These are bid to a contract. Later the deal is played with one player playing both defense hands. Scoring tables relate tricks bid to tricks made. Also for three players.

KINGS IN THE CORNER (Jax Limited). Players attempt to rid their hands of cards by playing to eight piles in descending rank and alternating colors.

A convenient tray keeps the piles in place, serves as a pot for chips, and holds the drawing deck. Two to 6 players.

PO-KE-NO (U.S. Playing Card), POKER-KEENO (Cadaco), POKER KENO (Whitman). Each player takes a board with pictures of twenty-five cards in a square. Cards are turned from a deck and chips placed on matching spaces. Five in a row wins, the amount depending on the Poker hand. Two or more players.

POKER ROYAL (Stancraft Products). Each player has an area on the board that ends with eight face-up cards. In turn a player can place a card from his hand into his own area or an opponent's. Poker hands win bonuses and pots in various ways. Two to 4 players.

SEQUENCE (Jax Limited). Playing a card from the hand allows placement of a chip on a matching board space. Jacks are wild, or anti-wild allowing removal of an enemy chip. Object is five-in-a-row. Two, 3, 4, 6, 8, 9, 10, or 12 players.

TEMPTATION POKER by Sid Sackson (Whitman). Ante for the first five cards. Then you can buy up to six more, the price going up steeply. But you can drop instead of paying. Choose your Poker hand from all the cards you hold. One to 6 players.

CARD GAMES (part II)—*where new decks of cards are used to play new games.*

BLACK SPY (Avalon Hill). Special deck with five colors and cards ranked from 11 down to 1. Play in tricks where either color or rank must be followed. Object is to avoid taking black cards, particularly the black "spies." Three to 6 players.

BRIDGETTE (Xanadu Leisure, Ltd.). Bridge for two, played with a regular deck expanded by three "colon" cards, which subtly affect the play. In bidding, players must reveal something about their holdings and in the advanced game "asking" and "cue" bids can force information.

DRAGONMASTER (Milton Bradley). Oversized cards have attractive drawings of Dragonlords, Warriors, Druids, and Nomads to replace the usual suits. Each player serves as the "dragonmaster," choosing a series of five "hands" where opponents are penalized for winning certain cards or tricks. Three or 4 players.

FLINCH (Parker Brothers). From a 150-card deck, with numbers from 1 to 15, each player is dealt a ten card "Flinch" pile. The object is to be the first to move the cards, in ascending order, onto center piles. Two to 8 players.

GRASS (Euro-Commerce). After playing a "Market Open" card, a player can add "Peddle" cards in various amounts to his "Stash." Opponents can play all kinds of nasty cards to stop him or to swipe what he has. Other cards give protection. And you can always make deals. Two to 6 players.

GREED (Whitman). Turn up a card and collect that money from the bank. A "greed" card allows an opponent's card to be drawn and the money collected from him; if not a money card you can try to bluff. Two to 6 players.

MAD MAGAZINE CARD GAME (Parker Brothers). Get rid of cards in your hand by matching previous discard in color, rank, or message. Message cards also allow some dirty tricks on opponents, but a "What me worry? You worry!" card can turn the tables. Two to 6 players.

MHING (Suntex International/Gelber Marketing). Mah Jongg, played with attractive cards instead of tiles. The scoring is somewhat simplified, and to make it even easier it is introduced in three levels. Two to 6 players.

MILLE BORNES (Parker Brothers). A novel race in which progress is made with distance cards. Opponents are slowed by hazard cards, such as "Flat-tire," to which either "Spare-tire" or "Puncture-proof" must be played to continue. A scoring system rewards skillful play. Two to 6 players.

NUCLEAR WAR (Flying Buffalo). Working from a hand of nine cards, players attempt to win over opponents' masses by propaganda or to kill them with nuclear attacks. Potent weapons can be exposed as a deterrent, but lose their surprise potential. Two to 6 players.

O.K. CORRAL (Discovery Games). To shoot you'll need one or more Bullet cards, followed by Turn, Reach, Draw, Aim, and Fire. A Miss card makes the bullet go astray and Ricochet sends it back against the shooter. Two or more players.

O'NO 99 (International Games). Cards run from 1 to 10 and the object is to avoid reaching ninety-nine or above. To help, there are cards that avoid adding to the total, that reverse the direction of play, and that make the next player play double. Two to 8 players.

PIT (Parker Brothers). A lively game where players, at the same time, trade commodity cards in an attempt to get a complete set, preferably in a more valuable commodity. Bull and bear cards add bonuses and penalties. Three to 7 players.

POWER PLAY (Task Force). Draw "leader" cards to try for control in seven areas—from Police to Press. Or take a chance on an "action" card. With control in one or more areas a Power Play can be attempted, a die throw giving the result. Two to 6 players.

RACK-O (Milton Bradley). Each player places ten cards in a rack in the order in which they are dealt. Then by drawing from the deck or the discard pile, he exchanges cards in an attempt to arrange them in numerical sequence. Two to 4 players.

ROOK (Parker Brothers). Cards of four colors run from 1 to 14, for a total of fifty-six. Rules for more than twenty games are included, some quite simple and others at the level of Bridge. One or more players.

RUBIK'S CUBE CARD GAME (Ideal). Pictures of cube faces with from zero to nine squares of four colors make up a forty-card deck. Players predict how many tricks they will win in each deal and score for being correct. Two to 6 players.

SKIP-BO (International Games). The deck consists of twelve each of 1 through 12 and twenty-four wild cards. Each player attempts to move cards from his "debit" pile to central piles, in ascending order. Hands and discard piles help. Two to 6 players.

THAT'S INCREDIBLE (MPH). A deck of eighty-one cards marked with letters, numbers from 1 to 27, slot machine symbols, and one of three colors is used for playing nine different games. Up to 27 players.

TURKEYS WILD! (HirschCo). Poker with a special deck that includes six wild cards. Play for points instead of chips. Each winning hand has a value, which is multiplied by the number of "bets" or "gobbles." Two to 6 players.

UNO (International Games). Get rid of your hand by playing to the top of the discard pile, matching the rank or the color. "Skip" cards pass the next player; "Reverse" changes the direction of play; "Draw" adds to an opponent's hand. Two to 10 players.

VENTURE by Sid Sackson (Avalon Hill). By strategic use of capital cards players gain control of corporation cards and organize them into profitable conglomerates. Proxy fights can capture key corporations from opponents. Two to 6 players.

WATERWORKS (Parker Brothers). Players separately attempt to connect a valve to a spout using pipe sections of different shapes and protection against leaks. Opponents try to cause leaks and other problems. Two to 5 players.

UNIQUE GAMES—*which, because of their equipment, their manner of play, or both, are one-of-a-kind.*

BE SHARP OR BE FLAT (Josets). Move your miniature metal instrument along a path of piano keys to the note specified by a card. If correct, collect "sharp" and "flat" cards. Win by completing a set of each. Two to 6 players.

BLACKOUT TIC TAC TOE (Ten Million Dollar Game Company). Nine tiles with X's and O's on the faces are placed in a square. A player flips them to his sign in accordance with numbers, or jokers, turned from a deck. Continue until a number already flipped shows. Score for threes in a row. Two players.

BLARF (Parlor Games). This stands for moving "Back, Left, Any, Right, Forward." Each player has a set of five pieces with these letters on one side and "A" on the other. A die is thrown, the player moves a piece that many spaces, and flips it. Capture by replacement or jumping. Two to 4 players.

BLOCKHEAD (Pressman). Using wooden blocks of different shapes players construct a tower. The object is to place a block so that the next player can't play without collapsing the structure. Any number of players.

BOOBY TRAP (Lakeside). Discs of different sizes are squeezed together by a spring-operated barrier. Players attempt to remove discs without disturbing the stress patterns. Failure causes a hand to rise. Any number of players.

BOOK OF LISTS GAME, THE (Avalon Hill). One hundred and twenty cards with lists of all kinds are provided—scrambled on one side, correct on the other. Players "bet" chips, each starting with his own color, on the correct position of an item. Chips as won fill a path toward a goal. Two to 4 players.

BREAD (EHP). Move around the board, taking cards with a suit mark or with one of four pictures. Bid for the right to turn a "bonus card" showing a combination of a suit and a picture. You collect if you hold cards that match. Two to 4 players.

CAN'T STOP by Sid Sackson (Parker Brothers). Columns are numbered from 2 to 12. Dividing throws of four dice allow markers to be entered and moved in three columns. Quit at any time and mark your progress, or lose it all with a throw that can't be used. Two to 4 players.

CHAIN REACTION (Hajjar International). Tiles with numbers from 1 to 15 are played to a many-hexed board. New tiles are added in numerical order, or against two or more that add up to the tile played. Letters on the other face of the tiles are for a similar word game. Two to 6 players.

DARK RIDERS GAME (Creative Prototypes Corporation). By dice throw players move one of three pieces along a series of paths, to capture the "moonstone" from a central tower. On the return home it can be stolen by an enemy piece, or can be returned to the tower by a "dark rider." Two to 4 players.

DARK TOWER (Milton Bradley). A combination of a board and electronic game. As players move through foreign kingdoms in search of three keys, their progress is measured by pressing buttons at the base of the tower and reading results of all kinds (including a continuing battle) in the window. One to 4 players.

DATAFLOW (Systems, Inc.). The board is a "flowchart" that appears complicated, but the logical design makes it easy to follow. Players attempt to reach spaces that add points to their "registers," the positioning of various "switches" affecting the movement. Two to 4 players.

DOUBLE TAKE (Cadaco). Square cards show pictures of four different objects. Each picture appears three times and another three are very similar. Cards are played by covering an identical picture, or by bluffing if you can get away with it. Two to 6 players.

DOWNFALL (Milton Bradley). Four sets of disks, numbered from 1 to 5, are manipulated through a series of five slotted vertical wheels. If a disk reaches the bottom out of numerical order it is eliminated. Two or 4 players.

DUPLIC (Knots). Each of two players has four pieces placed on a three by three field. In turn they move a piece to the vacant space, attempting to match the pattern on one of six cards they hold.

EXTINCTION (Carolina Biological Supply). A ruthless battle for survival between species. Each is defined by six different gene cards, and changing cards allows mutation to face new threats. Numbers on the tops of twenty dice per species keep track of the population. Two to 4 players.

FORTRAN (Orda/Educational Design, Inc.). The elements of how a computer program works are learned as players move through the program, entering values on three different "counters," and transferring results to their own "printers." Two players.

GINNY-O (Pressman, Chieftain Products). Using tiles representing playing cards, melds are played to the board in crossword fashion. However, there are nine possible starting spaces. Score for cards placed, spaces on the board, and for bringing a group to ten or more cards. Two to 4 players.

HEXAGONY (Avalon Hill). Each player battles with twelve pieces on a colorful field. They are moved according to dice throws and a player can continue throwing, giving up a supply unit each time. A turn can be used in an attempt to replenish the supplies. Two to 6 players.

HOG TIED (Selchow & Righter). Five numbered "pigs" move one space for each time their number shows on five dice. Captures are by passing or landing. After a pig becomes a "hog" it can go "wild" by throwing the dice as long as a hog face shows, accumulating the moves. Two players.

IMAGE (Avalon Hill). On a board images of known personalities are built, using cards specifying Time, Place, Activity, Status, and ending with the first initial of the last name. The player complet-

219

ing an acceptable image scores for the cards in it. Two to 6 players.

KING HAMLET (Gamevenings). Letters spelling KING HAMLET, with only one K and H, are hidden in various locations around Elsinore. Each player has a prince and a knight searching for a complete set. Duels are fought and assassins set by opponents can eliminate a piece. Two to 8 players.

MARRAKESH (Xanadu Leisure, Limited). By dice throw players set up six men on numbered spaces (like the home table in Backgammon). Hands of six cards from a special deck are played, the winner of a trick moving or removing his men. Bonuses are earned for certain sequences. Two players.

ON SETS (Wff 'N Proof). A game that is fun to play and helpful in teaching the concepts of Set Theory. The play is too complex (although some versions are suitable for young children) to be covered in this limited space. One or more players.

OVER-N-OUT (Gabriel). Players secretly place fifteen numbered cylinders into holes. Then in turn they lift one of the opponent's cylinders, returning it if not a 1. When a 1 is found the player continues for a 2, etc. Two players.

PUSH OVER by Alex Randolph (Parker Brothers). A slot in the plastic board provides a continuous track through which players move, attempting to push opponents over the edge. From one to three dice can be thrown, but there is a risk of having to start over. Two to 4 players.

PYRAMIDS & POLAR BEARS (Ten Million Dollar Game Company). Similar to Blackout Tic Tac Toe, except that there are sixteen triangular tiles with the titled objects on their faces. Score for various geometric shapes. In advanced version, tiles can be moved from their starting position. Two players.

Q-SETS (Orda/Educational Design, Inc.). Four different colored balls are randomly placed in a circle of eight pockets. Thirty cards show arrangements of the balls. Three are faced and players try to match one or more cards within three moves. Two to 4 players.

QUICKSAND (Whitman). Sand timers, four for each team, are moved across a board by a special die. An "S" allows flipping a friendly timer to gain sand, or an enemy to lose it. If sand runs out, a timer must start again. Two or 4 players.

QUIRKS (Eon Products). Strange plants and animals are formed from combinations of three cards. Players mutate their organisms to make them stronger, depending on the climate, which is constantly changing. One to 4 players.

RAMBLIN RHOMBOIDS (Ten Million Dollar Game Company). Similar to Blackout Tic Tac Toe, except that there are sixteen rhombus-shaped tiles with different colors on their faces. Score for various geometric shapes. In advanced version, tiles can be moved from their starting position. Two players.

RUBIK'S RACE (Ideal). A "Cube face" is set up by shaking nine colored dice into place. Each player shifts colored tiles, attempting to be the first to match the face in the center of a five by five area. Two players.

RUMMIKUB (Pressman). A set consists of 106 tiles: two each of numbers 1 through 13 in four colors, and two jokers. Play can be as simple as Rummy with cards. Another version allows melds to be rearranged; and one approaches Mah Jongg. Two to 4 players.

RUMMY-O (Cardinal). Similar to Rummi-kub, but only one form of play given.

STAY ALIVE (Milton Bradley). Fourteen intersecting strips form a seven by seven grid. Marbles are placed in the spaces. Sliding a strip opens holes, hopefully for your opponents' marbles and not yours. Two to 4 players.

STOP THIEF (Parker Brothers). Players move through streets and buildings in search of the thief, the electronic scanner giving clues by sound effects. Even if correctly located, he sometimes slips away with a horselaugh. Two to 4 players.

TANGOES (Rex Games). Tangrams are an old Chinese puzzle with seven pieces that fit together to form an endless variety of "pictures." Here two sets are provided, in an attractive package that serves as a display for the puzzle cards. One or 2 players.

THROB! (San Fiasco Productions). "Thrills" take the place of dollars as the currency. Mainly they are used to buy pieces of a broken heart. Confrontations occur, where thrills are won by the proper matching of passion, anger, caution, and guilt cards. Two to 6 players.

TRAK-CHEK (Pik VI Games). Players move checkers around a pair of bridge-connected tracks in accordance with the throw of special dice, which total only two or three. Capture by jumping over a single enemy. Two players.

TRI-NIM (Wff 'N Proof). The ultimate in Nim games (see page 92). Varying numbers of chips are set up in starting spaces and then moved toward three goal spaces. Each player attempts to be the last to move chips into a goal. Two or 3 players.

TRIVIAL PURSUIT (Horn Abbot Limited). One thousand cards, each with six questions/answers in six categories from "geography" to "sports & leisure." Move by die throw along a choice of paths, answer the category landed on, and continue if correct. Two to 6 players.

WFF 'N PROOF (Wff 'N Proof). A series of twenty-one games, of increasing difficulty, which are tied in with the study of modern symbolic logic. The play is quite different. One or more players.

WFF (Wff 'N Proof). The first two games of the Wff 'N Proof series sold separately. One or more players.

ZENN (Benander Games). A series of 101 different games played by flipping one or more chips along a waxed surface, rebounding against the raised edges, and landing in recesses at the ends. Two players.

*British manufacturers: Monopoly (Waddingtons), Diplomacy (Gibsons Games), Risk (Palitoy), The Mystic Wood (H. P. Gibson & Sons), The Sorcerer's Cave (H. P. Gibson & Sons), Careers (H. P. Gibson & Sons), Cluedo (Waddingtons), Mastermind (Invicta), Sorry! (Waddingtons), Boggle (Palitoy)